First World War
and Army of Occupation
War Diary
France, Belgium and Germany

41 DIVISION
123 Infantry Brigade
Queen's (Royal West Surrey Regiment)
11th Battalion
1 March 1918 - 30 September 1919

WO95/2638/5

The Naval & Military Press Ltd
www.nmarchive.com
Published in association with The National Archives

Published by

The Naval & Military Press Ltd

Unit 10 Ridgewood Industrial Park,
Uckfield, East Sussex,
TN22 5QE England
Tel: +44 (0) 1825 749494

www.naval-military-press.com

www.nmarchive.com

This diary has been reprinted in facsimile from the original. Any imperfections are inevitably reproduced and the quality may fall short of modern type and cartographic standards.

© **Crown Copyright**
Images reproduced by permission of The National Archives, London, England, 2015.

Contents

Document type	Place/Title	Date From	Date To
Heading	WO95/2638/6 11/Queen's (R.W. Survey) Mar' 18-sept' 19		
Heading	11th Battn. The Queen's Royal Regiment (West Surrey). March 1918		
War Diary	Italy	01/03/1918	02/03/1918
War Diary	France	03/03/1918	06/03/1918
War Diary	Ivergny	07/03/1918	21/03/1918
War Diary	Reference Map. Lens. 11.	22/03/1918	31/03/1918
Heading	41st Division. 123rd Infantry Brigade 11th Battalion The Royal West Surrey Regiment April 1918		
War Diary		01/04/1918	11/04/1918
War Diary	Ref Map Sheet 28 N.W.	12/04/1918	31/05/1918
War Diary	Ref Map Sheet 28	01/06/1918	27/06/1918
War Diary	Ref Map. Sheet 27.	28/06/1918	30/06/1918
Operation(al) Order(s)	11th Bn. "The Queen "S" Operation Order No. X. 1.	16/06/1918	16/06/1918
Operation(al) Order(s)	11th Bn. "The Queen's (R.W.S.) Regiment. Operation Order "X".	16/06/1918	16/06/1918
Operation(al) Order(s)	11th Bn. "The Queen's" Operation Order No. X. I.	17/06/1918	17/06/1918
Operation(al) Order(s)	11th Bn. "The Queen's" Operation Order No. X.II	19/06/1918	19/06/1918
Operation(al) Order(s)	11th Bn. "The Queen's" Operation Order No. X. III.	20/06/1918	20/06/1918
Operation(al) Order(s)	11th Bn. "The Queen's" Operation Order No. 5	26/06/1918	26/06/1918
Operation(al) Order(s)	11th. Bn. "The Queen's" Operation Order No. 6.	29/06/1918	29/06/1918
Miscellaneous	Instruction To Be Read In Conjunction With Operation Order No. 6.	29/06/1918	29/06/1918
Miscellaneous	Instruction To Be Read In Conjunction With Operation Order No. 7	29/06/1918	29/06/1918
Operation(al) Order(s)	11th Bn. "The Queen's" Operation Order No. 7.	30/06/1918	30/06/1918
Miscellaneous	Addenda To Operation Order No. 7.	30/06/1918	30/06/1918
Miscellaneous	June 30th 1918	30/06/1918	30/06/1918
War Diary	Ref Map. Sheet 28.	01/07/1918	31/07/1918
Operation(al) Order(s)	11th Batt. "The Queen's Operation Order No. 7.a	05/07/1918	05/07/1918
Miscellaneous	Instruction No. 78. Map Reference Sheet 26 S.W	10/07/1918	10/07/1918
Operation(al) Order(s)	11th Batt "The Queens" Operation Order No 8	10/07/1918	10/07/1918
Operation(al) Order(s)	11th Bn. "The Queen's" (RWS) Regiment. Operation Order No. 8.	16/07/1918	16/07/1918
Miscellaneous	Amendment To Operation Order No. 9. Dated 16-7-18	17/07/1918	17/07/1918
Miscellaneous	Addenda To Operation Order No. 9. Dated 16-7-18	17/07/1918	17/07/1918
Miscellaneous	Report On Raid. Carried Out By The 11th Queen's Regt.	19/07/1918	19/07/1918
Operation(al) Order(s)	11th Bn 'The Queens' Operation Order No 10.	20/07/1918	20/07/1918
Miscellaneous	Addendum to O/O No 10	21/07/1918	21/07/1918
Miscellaneous	Amendments To O.O. No 10.	21/07/1918	21/07/1918
Operation(al) Order(s)	11th. Batt. "The Queens" Operation Order No. 11.	25/07/1918	25/07/1918
Miscellaneous	Ref Operation Order No 11 dated July 25th 18	20/07/1918	20/07/1918
Operation(al) Order(s)	11th. Batt. "The Queens" Operation Order No 13	27/07/1918	27/07/1918
Operation(al) Order(s)	11th Batt "The Queens" Operation Order No 12	27/07/1918	27/07/1918
Miscellaneous	Addendum To Operation Orders No 13	28/07/1918	28/07/1918
Operation(al) Order(s)	11th Battn The. Queens Operation Order No 14.	31/07/1918	31/07/1918
Diagram etc	Appendix I		
Diagram etc			

Miscellaneous	Appendix II. Dress And Equipment.		
War Diary	La Clytte	01/08/1918	01/08/1918
War Diary	Zevecoten	02/08/1918	07/08/1918
War Diary	Lappe	08/08/1918	10/08/1918
War Diary	La Clytte	11/08/1918	29/08/1918
War Diary	Loye	30/08/1918	30/08/1918
War Diary	Tatinghem	31/08/1918	31/08/1918
Miscellaneous	Addendum To Operation Order No 15		
Operation(al) Order(s)	11th. Batt "The Queens" Operation Order No 15	01/08/1918	01/08/1918
Miscellaneous	Addendum To Operation Order No. 16. 11th Bn. "The Queen's" (RWS) Regt.	07/08/1918	07/08/1918
Miscellaneous	Addendum To Operation Order No. 16. 11th Bn. "The Queen's" (RWS) Regt.	07/08/1916	07/08/1916
Operation(al) Order(s)	Operation Order No. 16. 11th Bn. "The Queen's" (RWS) Regt.	07/08/1918	07/08/1918
Operation(al) Order(s)	Operation Order No. 17. 11th Bn. "Queen's" R.W.S. Regt.	08/08/1918	08/08/1918
Operation(al) Order(s)	Operation Order No. 17. 11th Bn. "The Queen's" Regt.	10/08/1918	10/08/1918
Operation(al) Order(s)	Operation Order No. 19. 11th Bn. "The Queen's" Regt.	12/08/1918	12/08/1918
Operation(al) Order(s)	Operation Order No. 20. 11th Bn. "The Queen's" Regt.	13/08/1918	13/08/1918
Miscellaneous	Battalion Orders. No. 2 By. Lieut. Col. W. L. Owen. M.C. Cmdg. 11th Bn. "The Queen's" Regt.	27/08/1918	27/08/1918
Operation(al) Order(s)	Operation Order No. 26. 11th Bn. "The Queen's" Regt.	28/08/1918	28/08/1918
Miscellaneous	Addendum To Operation Order No. 26	28/08/1918	28/08/1918
War Diary	Tatinghem	31/08/1918	02/09/1918
War Diary	Poperinghe	03/09/1918	27/09/1918
War Diary	Pulse Farm. Yoormezeele Klien Zillebeke.	28/09/1918	28/09/1918
War Diary	Wervicq Comines Railway	29/09/1918	30/09/1918
Operation(al) Order(s)	11th Bn "The Queens" Operation Order No. 30	08/09/1918	08/09/1918
Miscellaneous	Addendum To O.O. 30.	09/09/1918	09/09/1918
Operation(al) Order(s)	11th Bn. "The Queen's" Operation Order No. 32.	10/09/1918	10/09/1918
Operation(al) Order(s)	11th Bn "Queens" Operation Order No. 33	10/09/1918	10/09/1918
Operation(al) Order(s)	11th Queens Operation Order No. 31	10/09/1918	10/09/1918
Operation(al) Order(s)	11th Queens Operation Order No. 34	12/09/1918	12/09/1918
Miscellaneous	Ref O.O. No. 35	13/09/1918	13/09/1918
Operation(al) Order(s)	11th. Bn. "The Queen's" Operation Order No. 35	13/09/1918	13/09/1918
Operation(al) Order(s)	Operation Order No. 36. 11th Bn. "The Queen's" Regt.	18/09/1918	18/09/1918
Miscellaneous	Operation Order 11th Bn. "The Queen's" Regt.	24/10/1918	24/10/1918
Miscellaneous	1st Division A.	21/11/1918	21/11/1918
War Diary	Ypres	01/10/1918	01/10/1918
War Diary	Wervicq Menin Rly.	02/10/1918	13/10/1918
War Diary	Poulten Farm	14/10/1918	16/10/1918
War Diary	Courtrai	16/10/1918	19/10/1918
War Diary	Bossuvt	20/10/1918	25/10/1918
War Diary	Hustrit	25/10/1918	25/10/1918
War Diary	Avilghem Knokke	26/10/1918	31/10/1918
War Diary	Courtrai	01/11/1918	01/11/1918
War Diary	Knokke Area	02/11/1918	04/11/1918
War Diary	Berchem	05/11/1918	05/11/1918
War Diary	Berchem Sector	06/11/1918	08/11/1918
War Diary	Berchem & Mersche Area	08/11/1918	15/11/1918
War Diary	Geofferdinche	16/11/1918	17/11/1918
War Diary	Herinnes	18/11/1918	19/11/1918
War Diary	Stoqoy	20/11/1918	30/11/1918
Operation(al) Order(s)	Special Order No. 1 by Lieut Col W L Owen M.C. Commanding	17/11/1918	17/11/1918

War Diary	Stoqoy	01/12/1918	20/12/1918
War Diary	Braives	21/12/1918	31/12/1918
Heading	11th Bn Q.R. West Surreys 1919 Jan-1919 Sep		
War Diary	Seelscheid Area	08/01/1919	12/01/1919
War Diary	Seelscheid	13/01/1919	24/01/1919
War Diary	Lind	25/01/1919	31/01/1919
War Diary	Coln-Kalk	01/02/1919	31/03/1919
War Diary	Lindlar	01/04/1919	30/04/1919
War Diary	Engelskirchen Area	01/05/1919	07/05/1919
War Diary	Engelskirchen	08/05/1919	28/05/1919
War Diary	Ehreshoven	29/05/1919	30/06/1919
Operation(al) Order(s)	11th Battalion "The Queen's" (R.W.S.) Regiment Instructions To Accompany Operation Order No. 7.	19/06/1919	19/06/1919
Operation(al) Order(s)	11th Battalion "The Queen's" (R.W.S.) Regiment Instructions To Accompany Operation Order No. 7.	22/06/1919	22/06/1919
Operation(al) Order(s)	Operation Order No. 7. 11th Battalion "The Queen's" (Royal West Surrey) Regiment.	17/06/1919	17/06/1919
Miscellaneous	Administrative Instructions by Lieut. Colonel F.C. Longbourne. C.M.G. D.S.O. Comdg. 11th Battalion.	17/06/1919	17/06/1919
Miscellaneous	Composition Of Bus Column.		
Miscellaneous	Instructions To Accompany Operation Order No. 7.	18/06/1919	18/06/1919
War Diary	Ehreshoven	01/07/1919	15/07/1919
War Diary	Kalk	16/07/1919	30/09/1919

WO95/2638 (6)
11/Queen's (R.W.Surrey)
Mar '18 – Sept '19

123rd Inf.Bde.
41st Div.

Battn. with Bde. returned to France from Italy 1/6.3.18.

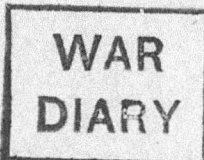

11th BATTN. THE QUEEN'S ROYAL REGIMENT (WEST SURREY).

M A R C H

1 9 1 8

WAR DIARY or INTELLIGENCE SUMMARY

Army Form C. 2118.

No ....

(Erase heading not required.)

Place	Date	Hour	Summary of Events and Information	Remarks and references to Appendices
ITALY.	Mch 28		Billetted at ST MICHELE. Entrained during the morning & proceeded to PADOVA goods station. Entrained proceeded to FRANCE. "C" & "D" Coys & Halves Batt. H.Qs. departed in first train at 12 noon. "A" & "B" Coys, remainder of Batt. H.Qs. & Transport departed by the second train at 4.0pm.	
	March 29		Travelling all day.	
	" 30		" " "	
	" 31		" " Crossed the French border.	
	" 1		" "	
	" 2		Detrained at DOULLENS, first train at 9am & second train at 2.30pm. Marched to billets at IVERGNY.	
FRANCE				
IVERGNY.	" 3		Cleaning kit & personal.	
	" 4		Coy. & platoon training in morning, recreational training in afternoon in vicinity of billets.	
	" 5		(Sunday) Brigade Church Parade (Cof E) in morning on Field Sof the IVERGNY - SUS-ST-LÉGER road.	
	" 6		Coy & platoon training in morning, recreational training in afternoon in vicinity of billets.	
	" 7		Battalion schemes in the vicinity of the SUS-ST-LÉGER - HUMBERCOURT road.	
	" 8		Company Schemes in the vicinity of billets in morning & recreational training in afternoon.	
	" 9		Coy work on ranges in FORÊT de LUCHEUX.	
	" 10		Coy work on ranges in FORÊT de LUCHEUX returning to billets in afternoon in vicinity of billets.	
	" 11		Coy & platoon training in morning & recreational training in afternoon in vicinity of billets.	
	" 12		Brigade scheme in vicinity of GRAND RULLECOURT and WARLUZEL.	
	" 13		(Sunday) Brigade Church Parade (Cof E) in morning on Field Sof the IVERGNY - SUS-ST-LÉGER road.	

WAR DIARY
or
INTELLIGENCE SUMMARY (2)

(Erase heading not required.)

Instructions regarding War Diaries and Intelligence Summaries are contained in F. S. Regs., Part II. and the Staff Manual respectively. Title Pages will be prepared in manuscript.

Place	Date	Hour	Summary of Events and Information	Remarks and references to Appendices
IVERGNY.	Jul 18"		Coy. Platoon training in vicinity of billets. 2 coy. took on ranges in FORET DU LUCHEUX.	
	" 19"		" " " " " " " "	
	" 20"		" " " " " " " "	
	" 21"		Marched to MONDICOURT, entrained at 2 pm, detrained at ACHIET-LE-GRAND, & afterwards marched to billets near by.	
REFERENCE MAP. LENS 11.	22"		Bn. marched to BIEFVILLERS when backs were dumped. Bn. marched to FAVREUIL, commenced digging at 8 pm. a line running N and S across the BAPAUME - CAMBRAI railway at about app: 800 x E of Sh N in ST-AUBIN. A & B coys on the N side - C & D coys on the S side. Bn. H.Q. was in a trench in advance of the left flank of the line, 200 x away. Transport remained at SAVOY CAMP 3 details at ACHIET-LE-PETIT. Digging stopped about 1 am & whole battalion proceeded to BEUGNY. Commenced digging new line about 1000 x N of BEUGNY running NW to the VRAUX - BEUGNY road. A & B coys in front line - C & D coys in support. At 7.30 am A & B coys bivouaced in extended order. To rejoin them the Royal Welsh Fusiliers who were on a line about 200 x in advance of the line being dug by A & D coys. Position is this vicinity were heavily bombarded during the morning & afternoon. The enemy employing rather a lot about 4.30 p.m. as the battalion on the right had been forced to withdraw. Orders came to this, A B & C coys withdrew through BEUGNY at 5.30 pm. They have no own extra artillery machine gun fire. It is reported by an M.O. that a great many of A & B coys were unable to reach the village owing to a heavy barrage by the enemy. The remnant of A, B & C coys were in garrison in BEUGNY 9 May. Got into position east of the village, the S of the village which was partly occupied. They	

WAR DIARY or INTELLIGENCE SUMMARY

Place	Date	Hour	Summary of Events and Information	Remarks and references to Appendices
	Mch 13th (cont)		remained in this position all night. When the enemy attacked at 4.30 pm. D Coy retired from their support position on to the BAPAUME – BEUGNY road where they reorganised & took up a position in Eastern starting that morning across the Railway. When the Battalion retired up to the Position N of BEUGNY. Batt. HQrs were made in the VAULX – BEUGNY road & according to the report of a S.B. runner, Batt HQrs were cut off at the same time as the position of A & B Coys on the retirement to the village. Casualties – Officers Killed. 2/Lt T.R. Cregeen M.C. Missing – Lieut Col. E. Otter M.G. Capt P.D. Henderson D.S.O. M.C. Capt A.C. Ryan M.C. Capt P.I. Poole M.C. (R.A.M.C.) Wounded Lieut G. Lansberne 2/Lt S.R. Pagan. C.G. Sidney. Other Ranks. Killed 5. Wounded 31. amongst Missing. 43.	2/Lt E.W. Spencer. " E.S. Brown. " A.C. Clenet. " L.R. Allen. 2/Lt A.J. McTiernan. Capt C.T. Royal.

INTELLIGENCE SUMMARY (4)

(Erase heading not required.)

Place	Date	Hour	Summary of Events and Information	Remarks and references to Appendices
	Mch 24		The position S. of BEUGNY was heavily bombarded from 9 a.m. to 10.30 a.m. The enemy on the right picket was in a dominant position. Batteries in use with our positions during the morning got to showing an enemy attack. About 12 noon Enemy made again bad to articulate so our own two picket had to be withdrawn to consolidate the battalion took up a position with the Cheshires on the left, running across the BAPAUME – CAMBRAI railway. The Ops [?] they were moved to another position in close line by the Cheshires when the performance all night, working on the trench. Transport moved to ACHIET-LE-PETIT.	
	Mch 25		The enemy attacked the position E. of BAPAUME about 10 a.m. & a fight which was more or less through on the left of the whole line was brilliant. During the retirement, the remainder of the battalion joined up with the 23rd Middlesex & on reaching ACHIET-LE-PETIT they were relieved by the 23rd Division. They then proceeded to BUCQUOY & reorganised. Transport moved to BUCQUOY. Marched to GOMMECOURT.	
	Mch 26		Marched to GOMMECOURT – Took up reserve position E. of village. Marched to BIENVILLERS in evening.	
	Mch 27		Transport moved to COUIN. Rested all day & night.	
	28			
	29		Resting all day & took up outpost position in evening at ESSARTS. Remained in outpost position all day [illegible]	J.S. Forrest

Place	Date	Hour	Summary of Events and Information	Remarks and references to Appendices
	Mch 29th (cont)		10th Royal West Kents & under the command of Major Wallace M.C. relieved one battalion of the 42nd Div. in front line N of ABLAINZEVELLE at 7½ am. Reinforcements reached joined battalion in front line at 9 am.	
	Mch 30th		" " " " in the line.	
	Mch 31st		" " " "	

E. A. Bowden
Major.
Commanding 1st Bn.

41st Division.
123rd Infantry Brigade

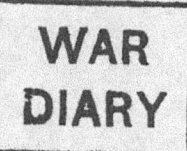

11th BATTALION

THE ROYAL WEST SURREY REGIMENT

APRIL 1918

WAR DIARY
or
INTELLIGENCE SUMMARY

Army Form C.2118.

(Erase heading not required.)

Instructions regarding War Diaries and Intelligence Summaries are contained in F.S. Regs., Part II. and the Staff Manual respectively. Title Pages will be prepared in manuscript.

No _____

12/3/41.

(1) 11 RW Surrey Regt

Vol 24

Place	Date 1914	Hour	Summary of Events and Information	Remarks and references to Appendices

Batt. in hut lines ABLAINZEVILLE, attached to 2 Bgde. Hut lines manned by 1 Coy Batt. M.G. Platoon at 10 pm by 2nd Lieut. Rawkins & BEAUMETZ. Detached from 10th Rnd. 5 Reorganised, to billets as ordered.

Casualties: Officers
Wounded: Capt. C. Fowler.
Other Ranks
Killed: 3
Wounded: 5

Entrained 3 am. Journeyed to billets at THIEVRES. Parties Reconnoitring opening. Entrained 9 am. Journeyed to billets at BEAUVOIR. Reached STEENVOORDE station at 10 pm. Entrained 12 midnight.

Detrained at POPERINGHE, entrained journeyed to billets S. of STEENVOORDE. Every kit & Personnel lost 20. Capt Turton arrived exchange Reinforcements arrived.

Brigade inspection by Corps Commander.

S.E.R. inspection by Brigade, Coy officers exchange, foraging inspection.

WAR DIARY
INTELLIGENCE SUMMARY. (2)

Army Form C. 2118.

Place	Date	Hour	Summary of Events and Information	Remarks and references to Appendices
	Jan 8th 1918	9 am	Marched to STEENVOORDE railway station (light railway), entrained & proceeded to POPERINGHE. Detrained & Awaiting Service. Marched to main station (full gauge) railway & entrained at 2.30 pm. Proceeded from POP to ST JEAN. Detrained & marched into YPRES. Billeted in cellars & dug-outs in centre of YPRES. Advance party proceeded from billets S. of STEENVOORDE to YPRES by motor bus in the afternoon & from there on to HASLER CAMP. Major Bowden M.C. assumed command.	
	9th		Clearing huts & re-organizing. 2 pm marched to HASLER CAMP. Billeted in huts.	
	10th		Clearing huts, working on improvements in the camp, working parties employed at night, loading trucks & unloading trucks to/from trains. Details marched back to BRAK CAMP. Bathroom & bathing arrangements at the camp. Shit trenches commenced in the vicinity of the camp. Loading & unloading parties supplied at night.	
	11th		" " " "	
REF. MAP	12th		Working on shit trenches & improving camp accommodation during the morning. Rest in the afternoon. Marched to battle zone at 5 pm. Occupied line of trenches running approximately from C.17.C.9.2, C.23.c.7.5. "C" & "D" companies in the front line, "A" company in support at BOSSAERT KEEP, "B" company in reserve & with Batt. HQrs at PICKLE HAUBE KEEP.	
SHEET 28 N.W.	13th		Continuous work in relief or support & reserve positions continues on R.E. supervision.	
	14th		" " " "	

WAR DIARY or INTELLIGENCE SUMMARY. (3)

Army Form C. 2118.

Place	Date	Hour	Summary of Events and Information	Remarks and references to Appendices
REFMAP SHEET 28 N.N	April 14 (cont.) 1916		Took up new line at 8 pm running approximately from C.28.d.9.4 to C.28.a.3.2. "D" & "A" Coys in the front line & "C" Coy in support at HASLER CAMP. B Coy remained as outposts on the evening of BOSSAERT KEEP & came under the command of Capt Hild. B.C. Outposts. Batt H.Q. moved to HASLER CAMP. Sentry groups were posted along the new line connecting the companies new in position.	
	15th		Continuous work on relays on posts in new line of resistance under the Supervision of the R.E. Batt H.Q. moved to artillery dug-outs at J.12 YPRES - ST JEAN road. J.3.a.7.8 in the evening. Working on front line & support posts under R.E. supervision.	
	16th		" " " " " "	
	17th		" " " " " "	
	18th		" " " " " "	
	19th		" " " " " "	
	20th		" " " " " "	
			New line of resistance slightly changed. "C" Coy moved their dug-outs in evening to take over UHLAN KEEP & JASPER KEEP. B Coy returned from outpost duty & took over "C" Coys position at HASLER CAMP. Line of resistance now :- JASPER KEEP, UHLAN KEEP, CARTE KEEP, & then to C.28.d.3.2. "C" & "A" Coys front line, "D" Coy support & "B" Coy reserve. Working on front line, support & reserve positions under R.E. supervision.	
	21st		Started between UHLAN KEEP & CARTE KEEP. Working all positions under R.E. supervision.	
	22nd		" " " "	
	23rd		" " " "	
	24th		" " " "	
	25th		" " " "	B Coy returned to outposts under command of Major Stallard M.C. B Coy relieved 7 Ca outposts & took up a later position.

WAR DIARY or INTELLIGENCE SUMMARY. (A)

Army Form C. 2118.

Place	Date	Hour	Summary of Events and Information	Remarks and references to Appendices
REF: MAP SHEET 28NW.	1915			
	26.8.15		Working on all positions under the R.E. Supervision during the day. No work 'C' Coy was doing was UHLAN & JASPER KEEPS & trench over a line from C28c94 to C28a32. CARTE KEEP trenches. "D" Coy relieved the 23rd Fusiliers in their positions running from C28a32 to I14.c.3.4. 'A' Coy, relieved the 20 R.F. 1 in their position running from I14.c.3.4 to I14.d.1.5 'B' Coy relieved the 10th Queens in their position running from I14.d.1.5 to WHITE CHATEAU exclusive, 6th our sector of the whole, conforms with these dispositions, 3 platoons in the front line & 1 platoon in support, & this line the means personal outposts line. The outposts under Major Stallard M.C. withdrew during our relief. Batt H.Q. remain	
	27		to Segments at the Junction of SAVILLE ROAD & the YPRES-POTIJZE ROAD I9a2.8. Work on position improvements during every facility. Our had formed sidings. Agreed allot. of ammunition was obtained. Every facility for was maintain throughout the day by our Stores Lewis Guns. The whole of our area has subjected to searching artillery fire. At dusk the two right companies were relieved by the 26 R.F. on completion of relief 'A' Coy went up & a position in support to 'C' Coy, approximately from C24d86 to C28c13. 9 'B' Coy went up & a position in support in support to D Coy, Appli. from C28c13. to I4a32. 'C' & 'D' Coy's boats returned at night, L/C N.O. Malcolm to original position at I3a7, 8. LB Col Robinson D.S.O. assumed command of divisional outposts.	
	28		Heavy artillery every active on our front line & support positions all day. CARTE KEEP was demolished & had to be evacuated during the morning. It was repaired & re-occupied at night. Considerable enemy movement was again observed the front line seats were able to find many good targets. One of the Patrols observed a trench lying in interest scrub S.E of CARTE KEEP. Work on all posts was carried ready day & night & the whole frontage was continually patrolled.	

Army Form C. 2118.

WAR DIARY
or
INTELLIGENCE SUMMARY. (5)

(Erase heading not required.)

Instructions regarding War Diaries and Intelligence Summaries are contained in F. S. Regs., Part II. and the Staff Manual respectively. Title pages will be prepared in manuscript.

Place	Date	Hour	Summary of Events and Information	Remarks and references to Appendices
REF: MAP SHEET 28NW.	Ap. 29ᵗʰ 1918		Front very quiet. Our posts received instructions for the new artillery barrage that is on. Work was carried out on all posts during the night & the whole front was continually patrolled. Bombing working parties were kept engaged until 4 A.M.	
	9 P.M.		Hostile artillery was very active on our support positions & throwing a patroon in left but Coy H.Q. was destroyed by shell fire about 9 P.M. Front line posts received some attention early in the night, but it was unmistakeably the key to reinforcements, enemy working parties heard & dispersed by patrols were kept up continuously.	

C Q Bowden
Major.
Commanding 11ᵗʰ Bn B. Queens.

WAR DIARY
or
INTELLIGENCE SUMMARY.

(Erase heading not required.)

Army Form C. 2118.

11 R.W. Group R
Vol 2

Place	Date	Hour	Summary of Events and Information	Remarks and references to Appendices
May	1st		The Battn were in area looking YPRES – V3. Whole Battn on working & loading parties. The area was	
	2nd		Shelled (gas) causing great discomfort. Casualties 1 OR Wounded	
	3rd		Nights killed nothing of the fighting having to be noted. Battn carried out on Reserve Lines, very little shelling during the day.	
	4th		The area was again heavily shelled. The Company moved to a safer position. Casualties 2 OR wounded	
	5th		Companies working the VLAMERTINGHE LINE have to leave work owing to shelling. Casualties 2 O Ranks Wounded	
	6th		½ Battn on working parties, the remainder cleaning reading. Day quiet. Casualties 1 OR Wounded	
	7th		Battn stand to, prepare man all positions. Little shelling by enemy. Casualties 1 OR Wounded	
	8th		Battn working parties all day, 2 Companies got to the Avara area for working at it.	
	9th		The Battn prepare to more into SIEGE CAMP B 21.c.0.3. snow at dusk. Casualties 10 Ranks Wounded	
	10th		The Battn is inspected by the CO by Companies. 2 OR proceed on working parties. Casualties 5 O Ranks Wounded	
	11th			

WAR DIARY or INTELLIGENCE SUMMARY.

Army Form C. 2118.

Place	Date	Hour	Summary of Events and Information	Remarks and references to Appendices
May	12th 13th		Men clean up & generally clear camp. Coys & Bn on working parties, men's dinners out daily. Very quiet.	
	15th		Orders for men in the evening. Batt. working the MARTINSART LINE. Forced to stop work by stelling. Casualties 1 O.R. wounded	
	16th		Covering parties go forward to take over from 18 KRRC in front line. Bn prepared to move into line at night	
	17th 18th		Relieved 18th KRRC on the night 17/18th. Hostile artillery active during early morning. Quiet during day. Positions Right Sub-Sector, Left Brigade, A 1st Division. 3 Companies in front line + Support. One in Reserve.	
	19th		Artillery M.G. Our patrols very active during night. Attempt to obtain identification unsuccessful. Enemy movement observed.	
	20th		I.10.c, I.11.d, I.11.b, I.11.c, I.12.c. Back areas shelled. Patrols active. Patrol occupied WEST FARM at H.10.c.8.2. from 2.30 a.m. to night fall. 1 O.R. killed	
	21st		Day very quiet. Relieved during night 21/22nd by 23rd Royal Fusiliers. Regt. went back to YPRES DEFENCES. Headquarters at RAMPARTS	
	22nd		Rested during day. Supplied working parties of 2 officers & 150 men & subsequently 3 officers + 250 O.Rs during night. Work	

WAR DIARY or INTELLIGENCE SUMMARY. No 3

Army Form C. 2118.

(Erase heading not required.)

Place	Date	Hour	Summary of Events and Information	Remarks and references to Appendices
	23rd 24th		Relieving FRONT & SUPPORT lines & making C.T. 2 O.Rs wounded. Work carried on as yesterday. 3 O.Rs wounded. Some wiring hastily entrified. YPRES DEFENCES cleaned up.	
	25th		Hostile artillery not maintaining same. Relieved 10th R.W. Kent Regt. in the Left Sub. Sector of Left Brigade. 41 O.Rs wounded during night 25/26th. Artillery very active on FRONT and SUPPORT lines between 9 a.m. and 12 noon. 2/Lt REYNOLDS-PARSONS killed, 2/Lt POTTER W. wounded, 7 O.R. killed, 19 O.R. wounded. Patrol sent out to M.H. & O.Ts.	
	26th			
	27th		Level reports obtained. Artillery active on vicinity of SUPPORT line. 2 O.R. wounded. Standing patrols & reconnoitring patrols sent out all night. Work started at DILLY FARM.	
	28th		Artillery normal. Many useful reconnaissance were carried out in the vicinity of DILLY FARM. Two officers patrols raided system of T head trenches at I.4.b.85 & found them unoccupied.	
	29th		Nothing of importance occurred during the day. Raiding party consisting of 3 officers 50 O.Rs left our trenches at I.4.d.2.8. to raid suspected post at I.5.c.5.6. Enemy were encountered. 3 enemy being killed by 2/Lt T.G. TREVELYAN, 2 others being accounted for by other members of the party. Patrol was caught in T.M. + M.G.	

WAR DIARY
or
INTELLIGENCE SUMMARY. № 4.

(Erase heading not required.)

Army Form C. 2118.

Place	Date	Hour	Summary of Events and Information	Remarks and references to Appendices
	29th/30th		Average. On return of patrol, 1 O.R. was found to be missing. Quiet day. Two patrols, both in charge of officers, reconnoitred vicinity of I.5.c.4.1. About 80 of the enemy entered trenches at DITHY FARM. On account of the size of the enemy party, patrol withdrew 1 Officer + 2 O.R. with the idea of enabling any single man returning later or German officer + his men. Attempts at entrance were made to catch them. This could not be done, but the German officer was killed in the struggle. The patrol commanded by 2/Lt MUSHETT. C. was then forced to withdraw by the rapid approach of a large party of the enemy attracted by the noise. Quiet during day. Usual reconnoitring & standing patrols out during night. Nothing to report.	
	31st			

W. T. Owen M.C.
County 11th Queens
Nothing Regt.

Army Form C. 2118.

WAR DIARY or INTELLIGENCE SUMMARY.
(Erase heading not required.)

11 R W Surrey (1)
Vol 26

Place	Date	Hour	Summary of Events and Information	Remarks and references to Appendices
REF MAP SHEET 28	June 1918 1st		Battalion in the line, left sub-sector Left Brigade. POTIJZE area. Advance party from 2/5 Yorkshires arrived & reconnoitred line.	
	2nd		Relief commenced. Relieved at night by the 2/5 Yorkshire Batt.	
	3rd		On completion of relief, the battalion proceeded by platoons to light railway crossing YOT VLAMERTINGHE CHATEAU. Conveyed by light railway to siding near LOUVE marched to camp. Batt. will remain in Brigade Reserve & march to PROVEN station.	
	4th		Entrained 7 a.m. & proceeded to HATTEN. Detrained 9 a.m. marched to billets in ST MOMELIN area. Batt. under orders of G.O.C. Batt H.Q. at LE PARADIS.	
	5th		Kit inspection & cleaning up. Baths.	
	6th		C.O.s inspection by Companies. Baths.	
	7th		Training under Company arrangements.	
	8th		" " " "	
	9th		Inspection of all companies by C.O. Church parade.	
	10th		Battalion marched to billets at TATINGHEM.	
	11th		Training under Batt. Programme	
	12th		Baths	
	13th		A & B Coys on range. C & D Coys training under Battalion programme.	
	14th		C & D Coys Batt H.Qs on range. A & B Coys training under Battalion programme.	

WAR DIARY or INTELLIGENCE SUMMARY

Army Form C. 2118.

Place	Date	Hour	Summary of Events and Information	Remarks and references to Appendices
	June 15th		Battalion Scheme. Church Parade. Non Station fire on range to carry on Divisional Competition.	
	16th		Battalion advance guard scheme.	
	17th		Battalion advance guard scheme.	
	18th		Brigade advance guard scheme.	
	19th		Batt'n "A" Platoon from C. Coy on range for Divisional Competition.	
	20th		Battalion scheme, acting as advance guard when encountered by the enemy.	
	21st		Battalion scheme in morning. Brigade horse show in afternoon.	
	22nd		Battalion on the range.	
	23rd		Church Parade. Remainder of day holiday.	
	24th		Organisation of Coys. Training under Coy arrangements.	
	25th		Marched to billets in ST MOMELIN area.	
	26th		" " in LEDRINGHEM area.	
	27th		Cleaning & inspections.	
Rt Map. SHEET 24	28th		Baths, gas drill & demonstration. S.B.R. tested by Bde Gas Officer. Advance parties sent	
	29th		Marched to Yprès L 28. Sin Acm met at BEAUVOORDE wood from 1-9 p.m. (?) Arrived in Yprès 9 p.m.	
	30th		Rested all day. Drew gasmasks. Paraded to relieve Right Front Batt. of the 104th Inf Bde. Marched to the line.	
				[signed] Lt Col. Commanding 1/5 Batt

SECRET. 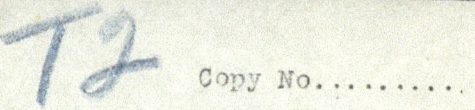 Copy No.........

11th Bn. "The Queen's" Operation Order No.X.1.

16th June 1918.

Ref: Map 27A.S.E. 1/20,000.

INFORMATION. 1. A German force is advancing from the direction of DUNKERQUE on ST.OMER. A German detachment estimated at one Regt. (3 Battns.) passed through ST.POLINCOVE last night.

INTENTION. 2. The Battalion will take part in a Brigade attack and will establish itself on the high ground between GRAND DISQUES and MORINGHEM. The Battalion frontage being from Q 26 c 9.5. to about Q 25 d 3.0.

3. The advance will be carried out by successive bounds as follows :-
1st bound. To the line W 5 a 1.9. W 4 a 7.4., W 3 d 6.3., W 2 c 7.5.
2nd bound. To the line Q 33 b 9.7., Q 32 c 0.0.,
3rd bound. To the line Q 27 a 0.3., Q 25 d 3.0.

DETAIL. 4. (a) The Battalion will move off as follows:-
Advance Guard. "A" Coy and Battalion Scouts. Commander H.C.Williams.
Main Body. Headquarters "B" and "C" Companies and "D" Company less 2 Platoons.
Rear Guard. Will be found by 2 Platoons of "D" Company.
(b) On word being received that the Advance Guard are in touch with the enemy in strength and are held up orders will be issued, and dispositions will be taken up as follows in Artillery Formation.
"B" Company. Right.
" C " " Left.
"D" " Reserve.
As soon as artillery formation is adopted the Rear Guard will be withdrawn.
(c) The 23rd Middlesex will co-operate on our Right, no-one on our left.
10th R.W.Kent - Right in Bde Reserve.
(d) Route. The Battalion will move via cross roads W 23 b 0.9. - LEULINGHEM - ZUDAUSQUES.
(e) Starting point - cross roads X 7 c 30.60.
(f) Time - 8.30 a.m.
The Main Body will not move from here until 10 a.m.

GUIDES. 5. The Intelligence Officer will send two guides to be at X 2 c 2.5. at 9.15 a.m. and two guides to be at X 7 d 4.9. at 9.15 a.m. to guide respect-ively 1 Sect. M.G.C. and 1 Sect. L.T.M.B. to the Main Body of the Battalion.

TRANSPORT. 6. (a) The first line transport will parade with the Battalion, on moving off it will report, less pack animals, to Lieut. SHRIMPTON 10th R.W.Kent Regt. at W 17 d 2.2. on TATINGHEM - SETQUES Road. Pack animals will move in rear of Main Body.
(b) The 2nd Line Transport will assemble under Lieut. HICKMAN 10th R.W.Surrey Regt. on road from X 8 a 9.8. to X 2 c 1.2. facing South, and will be in position by 9.30 a.m.

/ REPORTS. 7.

- 2 -

REPORTS.   7. 9   All reports to head of Main Body.
                    The Battalion Signalling Officer will gain
                    communication with Brigade Forward Party as soon as
                    possible.

LIAISON.   8. 5   Lieut. SANDERS will report to Headquarters 23rd
                    Middlesex Regt. and will keep the Battalion informed
                    of the situation on the right.

AID POST.   9. 6   CHURCH LENLINGHEM.

Issued by Runner
at 12 noon, 17/6/18

Copy No 1   C.O.
     No 2   2nd I/C
        3   A Coy
        4   B "
        5   C "
        6   D "
        7   123 Inf Bde
        8   23rd Middlesex
        9   10th R.W.Kents
       10   Q.M.
       11   T.O
       12   M.O
       13   Office
       14   Office
       15   War Diary

                                                    Capt. & Adjt.

SECRET.   Copy No...9......

11th Bn. "The Queen's" (R.W.S) Regiment.
OPERATION ORDER "X".

16th June 1918.

Ref: Map 27A.S.E. 1/90,000.

INFORMATION.   1.-   Small hostile patrols were reported by our
                     Cavalry on a line and about half way between
                     BARLINGHEM and CORMETTE at 2.0 p.m. 16th inst.
                     Otherwise no enemy movements are known.

INTENTION.   2.-   The Battalion will march to BARLINGHEM
                     tomorrow.

DETAIL.   3.-   (a) ADVANCED GUARD. - Commander Capt. H.C.
                     WILLIAMS, "A" Company.
                     (b) MAIN BODY. - Headquarters "B" and "C"
                     Companies, and "D" Company less 2 Platoons.
                         1st Line Transport.
                         Starting Point:- X 7 b 1.4. (Road almost
                                          opposite Battalion H.Q.
                                          billet).
                         Time:- 8 a.m.
                         Route:- TATINGHEM - LEULINE - CORMETTE.
                     (c) REAR GUARD. - Commander 2/Lieut. STRAWSON.
                     Two Platoons, "D" Company.

REPORTS.   4.-   Reports to head of Main Body.

                                                    Capt. & Adjt.

Issued by runner at 4 p.m.

                Copy No. 1. - "A" Coy.
                  "   " 2. - "B" Coy.
                  "   " 3. - "C" Coy.
                  "   " 4. - "D" Coy.
                  "   " 5. - Transport Officer.
                  "   " 6. - Quartermaster.
                  "   " 7. - 123rd Inf.Bde.
                  "   " 8. - Office.
                  "   " 9. - War Diary.

War Diary

SECRET.   Copy No. 15.

4th Bn. "The Queen's" Operation Order No. X.1.

17th June 1918.

Ref: Map 27A.S.E. 1/20,000.

INFORMATION.	1.	A German force is advancing from the direction of DUNKERQUE on ST.OMER. A German detachment estimated at one Regt. (2 Battalions) passed through ST.POLINCOVE last night.
INTENTION.	2.	The Battalion will take part in a Brigade attack and will establish itself on the high ground between GRAND DISQUES and MORINGHEM. The Battalion frontage being from Q 26 c 2.5. to about Q 25 d 5.0.
	3.	The Advance will be carried out by successive bounds as follows:- 1st bound. To the line W 5 a 1.9. - W 4 a 7.4. - W 3 d 6.3. - W 3 c 7.5. 2nd bound. To the line Q 33 b 9.7. - Q 33 c 0.0. 3rd bound. To the line Q 27 a 0.5. - Q 25 d 5.0.
DETAIL.	4. (a)	The Battalion will move off as follows:- Advance Guard. "A" Coy and Battalion Scouts, Commander Captain H.C.Williams. Main Body. Headquarters "B" and "C" Companies and "D" Company less 2 Platoons. Rear Guard. Will be found by 2 Platoons of "D" Company.

	(b)	On word being received that the Advance Guard are in touch with the enemy in strength and are held up, orders will be issued, and dispositions will be taken up as follows in Artillery Formation:-
		          "B" Company. Right.
		          "C" " Left.
		          "D" " Reserve.
		As soon as Artillery Formation is adopted the Rear Guard will be withdrawn.

	(c)	The 23rd Middlesex Regt. will cooperate on our Right, no one on our left. 10th R.W.Kent Regt. in Brigade Reserve.
	(d)	Route. The Battalion will move via Cross Roads W 33 b 0.9. - LEULINGHEM - ZUDAUQUES
	(e)	Starting Point. Cross Roads X 7 c 30.80.
	(f)	Time. 8.30 a.m. The Main Body will not move from cross roads until 10.0 a.m.
LIAISON.	5.	Lieut. SANDERS will report to Headquarters 23rd Middlesex Regt. and will keep the Battalion informed of the situation on the Right.
AID POST.	6.	CHURCH LEULINGHEM.
GUIDES.	7.	The Intelligence Officer will send two guides to be at X 9 c 3.5. at 8.15 a.m. and two guides to be at X 7 d 4.4. at 8.15 a.m. to guide respectively 1 Section Machine Gun Corps and 1 Section Light Trench Mortar Battery to the Main Body of the Battalion.
TRANSPORT.	8.	(a) The 1st Line Transport will parade with the Battalion; on moving off, it will report less pack animals, to Lieut.SHRIMPTON 10th R.W.Kent Regt. at N 17 d 6.2. on ST.MARTIN - TATINGHEM - LE FOSSE FARM Road. Pack animals will move in rear of Main Body.

/8. (b)

8. (b) The 2nd Line Transport will assemble under Lieut. HICKMAN 11th Bn. "The Queen's" Regt. on road from X.8.a.9.8. to X.9.c.1.2, facing South, and will be in position by 8.30 A.M.

REPORTS. 9. All reports to head of Main Body.
The Battalion Signalling Officer will gain communication with Brigade Forward Party as soon as possible.

10. ACKNOWLEDGE.

(Sgd) C.J.M.PAIGE.

Capt. & Adjt.

Issued by runner at 12 noon 17-6-18.

```
Copy No.  1.  -  C.O.
   "   "  2.  -  2nd i/c.
   "   "  3.  -  "A" Coy.
   "   "  4.  -  "B"  "
   "   "  5.  -  "C"  "
   "   "  6.  -  "D"  "
   "   "  7.  -  123rd Inf. Bde.
   "   "  8.  -  23rd Middlesex Regt.
   "   "  9.  -  10th R.W. Kent Regt.
   "   " 10.  -  Quartermaster.
   "   " 11.  -  Transport Officer.
   "   " 12.  -  Medical Officer.
   "   " 13)
   "   " 14)  -  Office.
   "   " 15.  -  War Diary.
```

SECRET. Copy No. ....

11th Bn. "The Queen's" Operation Order No. X.II.

14th June 1918.

Ref: Map 27A.S.E.1/20.000.

INFORMATION.
(enemy). 1. (a) The enemy hold an Outpost Line very thinly, on a line running through NOIR CARME - ZUDAUSQUES - CORNETTE. The enemy's main line of Outposts is the line QUELMES - LEULINGHEM - ETREHEM.

(Ours). (b) The Brigade will be billeted in PT.DIFQUES on the night of the 19th/20th inst. Our covering troops are on the high ground between MORINGHEM and GD.DIFQUES.

INTENTION. 2. (a) Our covering troops, early tomorrow morning, will push forward and endeavour to oust the enemy from his thinly held Outpost Line and force him back to his Main Line of Outposts.
(b) The Battalion will march to AUDENTHUN and will be prepared to attack LEULINGHEM at short notice.
(c) Should our covering troops fail to drive in the enemy's Outposts then the Battalion will attack this line, clear the way and proceed to AUDENTHUN.

DETAIL. 3. (a) Order of march:- Scouts, "B" Coy., B.H.Q., "C" "D" and "A" Coys.
Advance Guard:- Battalion Scouts and "B" Coy.
Commander - Captain F.S.RIDER.
(b) There will be no troops co-operating immediately to our left or right.
(c) Route:- PT.DIFQUES - MORINGHEM - BARLINGHEM - NOIR CARME - ZUDAUSQUES - AUDENTHUN.
(d) Starting Point:- CHURCH MORINGHEM.
(e) Time:- 11 a.m.

TRANSPORT. 4. Instructions to be notified later, except for pack animals which will be with their Coys.

REPORTS. 5. Head of main body.
In the event of Battalion having to deploy and attack - all reports will be sent to b 48.40 Road junction BARLINGHEM. Q31

(Sgd) C.J.M.PAIGE.
Capt. & Adjt.
11th Bn."The Queen's" Regt.

Issued by runner at 4.30 p.m.

Copy No. 1. - C.O.
" " 2. - 2nd i/c.
" " 3. - "A" Coy.
" " 4. - "B" "
" " 5. - "C" "
" " 6. - "D" "
" " 7.) - 123rd Inf.Bde.
" " 8.)
" " 9. - Quartermaster.
" " 10. - Transport Officer.
" " 11. - Medical Officer.
" " 12. - Office.
" " 13. - File.
" " 14. - War Diary.

SECRET.   Copy No. 2

11th Bn. "The Queen's" Operation Order No.XIII.

30th June 1918.

Ref: Map 27A.S.E. 1/20,000.

INFORMATION.   1.   The enemy hold the line running through BOISDINGHEM -
                    Q 32 d 99.30 - CORNETTE - TILQUES.
                    This line appears to be held in strength.

INTENTION.   2.(a)The Battalion will take part in a Divisional Attack
                    on the above line on the morning of the 21st inst.
                 (b)The Battalion frontage is approximately 1000 yards,
                    and runs from Q 32 c 50.00 to Q 33 Central.

DETAIL.   3. (a)Right - "D" Company.
                     Centre- "B"   "
                     Left - "C"   "
                     Reserve-"A"   "
                 (b)Each Company frontage is about 350 yards.
                 (c)It is not intended, nor is it considered necessary,
                    that there should be an attack of one continuous line
                 (d)The 16th Queen's will attack on the Right and the 18th
                    Middlesex on the Left.
                 (e)ASSEMBLY. The Battalion will assemble on the
                    BARLINGHEM - CORNETTE ROAD.(Q 31 b 45.30 to Q 32 a 99.25)
                 (f)Time. 10.30 a.m.

TRANSPORT.   4.   Instructions to be notified later except for pack
                    animals which will be with their Companies.

REPORTS.   5.   All reports will be sent to BARLINGHEM ROAD JUNCTION
                    Q 31 b 45.30.
                    There will be a Signal Receiving Station at the
                    WINDMILL, Q 26 c 90.10.

                                              (Sgd) C.J.M.PAIGE.
                                                   Capt. & Adjt.
                                              11th Bn."The Queen's" Regt.

          Issued by runner at 8 p.m.

               Copy No. 1. - C.O.
                "   "   2. - 2nd i/c.
                "   "   3. - "A" Coy.
                "   "   4. - "B" "
                "   "   5. - "C" "
                "   "   6. - "D" "
                "   "   7.)
                "   "   8.) - 193rd Inf.Bde.
                "   "   9. - Quartermaster.
                "   " 10. - Transport Officer.
                "   " 11. - Medical Officer
                "   " 12. - Office.
                "   " 13. - File.
                "   " 14. - War Diary.

S.E.C.R.E.T.   Copy No. 12

War Diary

11th Bn. "The Queen's" Operation Order No. 5.

26th June, 1918.

Ref. Map Sheet 17 Scale 1/40,000.

The Battalion will move today to the ARNEKE AREA.

PARADE. 1. The Battalion will parade at 10 a.m., Head of Column opposite Crucifix on the Corner by the old Battalion Parade Ground.

ORDER OF MARCH. 2. B.H.Q., "A", "B", "C" and "D" Companies.

DRESS. 3. Full Marching Order.

DISTANCES. 4. Between Companies, Transport, etc. as for yesterday.

5. All Officers' Valises, Company Stores to be outside Company H.Q. by 8.30 a.m.
Mess Kit to be outside Company H.Q. by 8.45 a.m. for loading.

BILLETS. 6. Billets to be left perfectly clean - certificates to this effect to be in Battalion Orderly Room by 9.30 a.m.

7. Marching Out States to be in Battalion Orderly Room by 9.30 a.m.

8. Falling Out States to be sent to the head of the Column.

9. All lorries should take different routes from the marching troops, and when finished with in the evening will report back to Motor Transport Company.

10. A representative of the Battalion to meet the Brigade Supply Officer at Cross Roads I 8 @ 4.3. at 9.30 p.m.

(Sgd) C.J.M.PAIGE.
Capt. & Adjt.
11th Bn. "The Queen's" Regt.

Issued by runner at 7 a.m.

Issued to all recipients of Operation Order No.4.

SECRET.   Adjutant   Copy No. 3

11th Bn. "The Queen's" Operation Order No. 6.

29th June 1918.

Ref. Map Sheet 27.

INTENTION. 1.   The Battalion will move to the "Y" Area L 28 d. today.
                 The march will be made in two stages, halting for
                 dinners about 1.30 p.m. and arriving in "Y" Area at
                 dusk.

DETAIL.   2.   (a) Order of March :- B.H.Q., "D", "C", "B" and "A" Coys.
                 Parade :- Battalion will parade on the main CASSEL Road.
                 Starting Point :- Head of Column at junction of roads
                 at I 8 c 99.50 facing S.E.
                 Time :- 9 a.m.(watches will be synchronised on 9 a.m.
                        parade).
                 Route :- ZERMEZEELE, HARDIFORT, RYVELD, STEENVOORDE,
                          ABEELE, ABEELE STATION.

                 (b) A long halt will be made in the vicinity of BOIS de
                 BEAUVOORDE (K 33 b) for dinners. Major BOWDEN will
                 proceed ahead to select a suitable place.
                 After dinners, Major BOWDEN with 1 N.C.O per Coy.
                 mounted, will go forward and select the most concealed
                 places for bivouacing in "Y" Area.
                 Normal halts and distances will be observed on the
                 march.

                 (c) BAGGAGE All baggage including men's packs (except
                 those men attending sick parade) will be dumped at
                 each Coy.H.Q. as follows:- "A" Coy 7 a.m. "B" Coy
                 7.15 a.m. B.H.Q. 7.45 a.m. "C" Coy 8.15 a.m. "D" Coy
                 8.30 a.m. Officers and men will have their valises
                 and packs tonight.
                 Mess Cart will call with baggage wagon.

                 (d) Sick Parade :- "A" & "C" Coys 7.15 a.m.; "B" & "D"
                 Coys 7.30 a.m.

                 (e) Advance Parties. The Advance Parties, as detailed below,
                 will report at ARNEKE CHURCH at 5.45 p.m. today. They
                 will be picked up by lorry and proceed to L 28 c 9.2.
                 where they will report to the Commandment I.D. at
                 9.30 p.m. The unexpired portion of the day's rations
                 and one complete day's rations will be carried.
                 Officers will find it inconvenient to carry large
                 trench bundles. The Advance Party will report at
                 "A" Coy's H.Q. at 9.30 a.m. for further instructions,
                 from the C.O.
                 Advance Party will consist of 4 Coy Commanders (Lieut.
                 SANDERS for "B" Coy), 1 Platoon Sergeant per Platoon,
                 and 2 guides per Coy, Sergt Sparrow, L/Cpl Saddler, Pte
                 Conlyn and Cpl. Newman for B.H.Q.

                 (f) Supplies. The supply wagons will draw from the present
                 dump today (29th) at 1.30 p.m. and will rejoin the
                 Battalion immediately in "Y" Area. The Signalling
                 Sergt. and Cpl. Scowan both supplied with maps, will be
                 sent to guide the above wagons to "Y" Area.

REPORTS.   3.   To head of column.

                                            (Sgd) C.J.M.PAIGE.
                                                  Capt. & Adjt.
                                            11th Bn. "The Queen's" Regt.

                 Issued by Cyclist Orderly at 5.30 a.m.

```
Copy No.  1.  - C.O.
 "    "   2.  - 2nd i/c.
 "    "   3.  - Adjutant.
 "    "   4.  - 123rd Inf.Bde.
 "    "   5.  - "A" Coy.
 "    "   6.  - "B"  "
 "    "   7.  - "C"  "
 "    "   8.  - "D"  "
 "    "   9.  - Signalling Officer.
 "    "  10.  - Transport Officer.
 "    "  11.  - Quartermaster.
 "    "  12.  - Medical Officer.
 "    "  13.  - R.S.M.
 "    "  14.  - File.
 "    "  15.  - War Diary.
 "    "  16.  - Spare.
```

INSTRUCTIONS to be read in conjunction
with Operation Order No.6.

SICK PARADE. "A" and "C" Coys at 7.15 a.m.
"B" and "D" Coys at 7.30 a.m.
All men parading sick will report punctually at the above hours in Full Marching Order. Company Commanders will ensure that all men attending sick parade have ample time to have good breakfast. Men not being evacuated will rejoin their Companies at the Assembly Point.

ADVANCE PARTY. Officers, N.C.Os and O.R's detailed for Advance Party will dump their packs and valises with those of their companies and will proceed in Battle Order, minus Great Coats. The Advance Party will be under the command of Captain Lansdowne. They will report at ARNEKE CHURCH at 5.45 p.m. on night of 29th/30th, and will eventually report to Commandment ID. at L 29 c 9.2. at 9.30 p.m. They will carry the unconsumed portion of the day's ration and one whole day's rations in addition. The Advance Party will meet the C.O. at "A" Coy's billet at 9.30 a.m. on morning of 29th instant, for further instructions. Company Commanders will therefore have time to see their Companies as far as the Assembly Position. 2nds in Command will ride Company Commanders' Chargers.

ROUTINE. Reveille 5.30 a.m. Breakfast 6.15 a.m.
Battalion Parade 9.0 a.m. Starting Point I 8 c 99.60.
Head of Column at junction of roads facing S.E.
Order of March - B.H.Q., "D", "C", "B", and "A" Companies.
Dinners will be served in the field about 1.30 p.m. at K 33 Central if fine, but if wet in the ABEELE AERODROME.
Teas at 5.30 p.m. at same place.
Battalion will proceed to bivouac camp L 28 Central reaching there at dusk.
Major BOWDEN and 1 N.C.O. per Company mounted will proceed after dinner to "Y" Camp (L 28 d), and will make full arrangements to bivouac the Battalion during the night at this camp.
Transport will accompany the Battalion as far as L 26 Central and then will proceed to "A" Camp in L 21 d. Transport Officer will send forward his mounted sergeant to make necessary arrangements.

Sentry. The Adjutant will arrange to mount a sentry at junction of roads L 34 d 00.40.(DREEF). This sentry will be posted as a guide to anyone wanting the Camp and also to guide the Brigade Despatch Rider who will call at the camp for despatches at 9.0 p.m.

MOVEMENT. Every possible means will be taken to keep the relief of the French in the line by this Division secret. There will therefore be no movement on a line running N. and S. through grid 31, 32 (Sheet 28), until after dusk. i.e. 9.30 p.m. When in bivouac for the night in "Y" Camp all ranks will take every advantage of cover in the way of huts, hedges, trees, etc., and there will be as little movement as possible whilst the Battalion is in this camp. There will be no lights for officers and men except in Battalion H.Q. at all during the stay in the bivouac camp. There will be no fires of any description. By day one officer per Company and one per Battalion H.Q. will be on duty to see that these precautions are fully carried out. One A.A.Sentry per Company will also be on duty to warn the approach of enemy aircraft. One Lewis Gun per Company will be mounted for A.A. purposes, but it will not fire unless the troops are attacked by aircraft. It will be fully explained by Company 2nd i/c's to all ranks that this secrecy is not a matter of "wind up", but owing to this somewhat difficult relief it becomes a matter of very necessary military precautions.

/ S.A.A.

S.A.A. 60 boxes of S.A.A. are being taken up to each Battalion H.Q. by the French Troops. The necessary distribution of this ammunition will be made from B.H.Q. In addition every N.C.O and man will carry up a bandolier of 50 rounds. This will be collected and made into Platoon Dumps in the line.

Very Lights. Every man will be handed two Very Light Cartridges, similarly, platoon dumps will be made of these.

S.A.A. and Very Lights will be distributed in "Y" Camp.

BOMBS. To be notified later.

Cooking. There will be no cooking in the line - all food and tea will be cooked at the Transport Lines and sent up to B.H.Q. where it will be drawn and distributed by "B" Company. "B" Company Commander will therefore make all necessary arrangements.

C.Q.M.S's. 2 C.Q.M.S's will report nightly. "C" & "D" and "A" & "B" C.Q.M.S's will work both companies on alternate nights.

Lewis Guns. Six Lewis Guns will be taken in the line by each Coy. 20 filled magazines will be taken. (for each gun).

The main thing for Company Commanders to bear in mind is that there is every possibility of attack and no effort will be spared to ensure that their commands understands in detail all instructions.

29th June 1918.

(Sgd) C.J.M.PAIGE.
Capt. & Adjt.
11th Bn. "The Queen's" Regt,

INSTRUCTIONS No.7 to be read in conjuction with
Operation Order No. 7.

(a) There will be as little movement as possible whilst in this area.
(b) All ranks including Officers will have one hours gas drill today.
(c) Opportunities will be taken by Platoon Commanders to talk to their Platoons on the work on hand, trench discipline, counter attack work, a necessity of working hard all night, resting by day.
(d) Instructions No. 6 issued with Operation Order No. 6 will be carefully studied by all officers.
(e) Operation Order No.7 will be thoroughly explained to all ranks by their Platoon Commanders.
(f) In the event of shelling whilst on the march to the line, Platoon Commanders will on no account allow their platoons to become disorganised, nor will they delay progress. Owing to the shortness of the night it is essential that the relief is carried out quickly.
(g) Each Platoon, each Coy H.Q. and Bn.H.Q. will hold themselves responsible for carrying their own food for the following day, i.e. the first day in the line. It will be already cooked, and will be put together in sandbags, each sandbag about half full. All Platoon Commanders must recognise their responsibility in this direction, and will therefore march in rear of their platoons for this and the reason mentioned in para (f) above.
(h) All water bottles will be filled with cold tea. This will not be drunk during the night; it is the following day's ration.
Battalion H.Q. will endeavour to carry up a further supply, but this is very doubtful, and no reliance may be placed upon it.
(i) All men who are not going in the line with the Battalion will remain with the baggage of their respective Companies until after the Battn. has moved. They will then receive orders from Captain PAIGE.
(j) LEWIS GUNS. Lewis Guns and Panniers will be issued from the limbers as soon as the Companies leave the road for the cross-country track. Every care must be taken to avoid delay. Battalion H.Q. will notify when this distribution is to take place.
Panniers will be ready filled, 8 filled magazines in each set of Panniers. During the morning all magazines will be thoroughly cleaned and overhauled.
(k) S.O.S.ROCKETS. The French S.O.S. Signal will be taken over and taken into use on relief. Our own S.O.S. Signal, Red over Red over Red will come into use at 3.a.m. July 2nd, and then all French S.O.S. lights will be collected and returned to Battn. H.Q..
(l) WATER. The water supply in the forward area is doubtful. Full Instructions will be issued in regard to this later.
(m) R.E. STORES. Indents will be forwarded to Battn. S.A.H.Q. without delay on taking over the line.
(n) TRANSPORT. Transport will not proceed further EAST than M.19.b.0.3. unless otherwise ordered. This is the Battn. dump. By day it will not proceed further EAST than the N. & S. Grid line running through squares 31 & 32. (Sheet 36).
(o) S.A.A. One extra Bandolier per O.R. will be carried on the man to the line as previously ordered. 30 Boxes of S.AA. will be at M.S.S.3.0. The distribution will be as follows:-
One box per platoon = 16. 2 boxes per Coy. H.Q. = 8.
30 boxes at Bn.H.Q. = 26. -- Total 50.
This will be looked upon as Reserve S.A.A. and must be kept to strength. This is also L.G. Reserve.
(p) MEDICAL ARRANGEMENTS. All cases will be sent direct to the Battn. R.A.P.
(q) STRETCHERS. All Coy and H.Q. stretchers will be carried to the line by the Stretcher Bearers.
(r) SICK PARADE. At Bn.H.Q. nightly immediately after Stand Down.
(s) STAND TO. Stand To at nights will commence half an hour before dusk and continue for half an hour after. Stand To in the Morning will commence one hour before dawn and continue for one hour. During both Stand To's a thorough box helmet inspection will be carried out. They will be worn by Platoon Commanders and O.R. for at least 10 minutes at each Stand To.

/Rifles

(continued)

Rifles and S.A.A. will be cleaned and inspected at each Stand To. Lewis Guns will be cleaned and inspected at least twice in each 24 hours, care being taken to regulate their cleaning so that only one gun in each Coy. is stripped at any one time.

                                          (Sgd) C.J.M.PAIGE.
                                                Capt. & Adjt.
29th June 1918.   11th Bn. "The Queen's" (R.W.S) Regt.

SECRET.   Copy No...... 16

11th Bn. "The Queen's" Operation Order No.7.

                        26   30th June 1918.

Ref. Map Sheet 27 & 21.

INFORMATION.   1.   (a) The 124th Inf.Bde is relieving the French troops on
                        our Right tonight and also on the night 1st/2nd
                        July.
                    (b) The 122nd Inf.Bde those on our Left, on the same
                        nights.
                    (c) The relief of the French Artillery by our own will be
                        completed by the morning 2nd July.
                    (d) Tonight "B" Coy. 41st Divl.M.G.Battn. will take over
                        from the French M.G.'s on this Battalion's front, with
                        four guns.
                    (e) One French officer per Coy. and one for B.H.Q. will
                        remain in the line for 24 hours after relief.

INTENTION.   2.   The Battalion will relieve the PESSEMESSE 104th Regt.
                    in Support tonight.

DETAIL.   3.   (a) Order of March :- B.H.Q., "C", "D", "A" & "B" Coys.
                        Platoons will move in file at 100 yards distance.
                    (b) Parade :- The Battalion will parade at the bottom
                        of the Camp, "C" and "D" Coys. behind the "cooker"
                        hedge, "A" Coy. by the E Hedge, "B" Coy. by the
                        W Hedge.
                    (c) Starting Point :- Camp Gate.
                        Time :- 9.0 p.m.
                        Dress :- Battle Order less great coats.
                        Route :- L 35 d 1.3 & as guided by guides.
                        Guides :- Guides will be picked up at L 35 d 1.3.
                    (d) Baggage :- All baggage, including men's packs with
                        great coats will be stacked in the vicinity of the
                        Coy. Parade Grounds. Any men sick or otherwise who
                        will not be going in the line with Battalion will be
                        left in charge of each Coy's baggage.

TRANSPORT.   4.   Lewis Gun Limbers will accompany their respective
                    Coys., marching with the leading platoon of each Coy.
                    One Limber will march with Battalion H.Q. and will
                    carry S.A.A., Bombs and Very Lights, & Certain stores
                    including reserve of box helmets and 20 tins of
                    cold tea.

REPORTS.   5.   All reports to head of Battalion.

COMPLETION   6.   On completion of relief each Coy. Commander will
OF RELIEF.   immediately send same through by runner to Battalion
                    H.Q.

                                              (Sgd) C.J.M.PAIGE.
                                                    Capt. & Adjt.

              Issued by runner at   m.
              Copy No. 1. - C.O.   Copy No. 9. - Signalling Offr.
               "   " 2. - 2nd i/c.   "   " 10. - Transport Offr.
               "   " 3. - Adjutant.   "   " 11. - Medical Offr.
               "   " 4. - 123rd Bde.   "   " 12. - R.S.M.
               "   " 5. - "A" Coy.   "   " 13. - Quartermaster.
               "   " 6. - "B" Coy.   "   " 14. - File.
               "   " 7. - "C" Coy.   "   " 15. - War Diary.
               "   " 8. - "D" Coy.   "   " 16. - Spare.

ADDENDA TO OPERATION ORDER No. 7.

INFORMATION.   The 123rd Inf. Bde. will relieve the
               104th French Regt. in the Centre Sector
               of the 7th French Divisional Front.

                              (Sgd) C.J.M.Paige.
                                    Capt. & Adjt.
30th June 1918.   11th Bn."The Queen's"(R.W.S) Regt.

To Ass. Adj. June 30th 1918

Instructions No 7 Part 2 to be read in conjunction with operation orders No 7.

A. The 174th Infantry Brigade on our right will have 20th Durham L.I. in the Front line, 26th R. Fusiliers in Support, and 10th Queens in Reserve.

B. The 172nd Infantry Brigade on our left will have 15th Hampshire Regt. in the Front line, 18th K.R.R.C in Support and the 12th East Surrey Regt. in Reserve.

C. The following will be locations of Brigade and Battalions of the Brigade on completion of relief :—

    Brigade H Q   M.6.c.30.40.
    11th Queens   M.12.C.8.1.
    10th R.W. Kents   M.5.a.25.50.
    23rd Middlesex Regt N.7.c.2.3.
    173rd L.T.M.B.   "Y" Bivouac Area.

for Capt & Adjt
Batt. Ord. Room

WAR DIARY of 1st Batt. The Queens

INTELLIGENCE SUMMARY.

Army Form C. 2118.

Place	Date 1918	Hour	Summary of Events and Information	Remarks and references to Appendices
Ref Map Sheet 28.	July 1st		Relief of the 10th Queens by 1st Regt in support positions at the Cable section, SCHERPEN-BERG – LA CLYTTE LINE, completed at 1.30am. Hostile M.G. fire very active during the hours of darkness. 23rd Middlesex relieved French troops in front line positions with Slight shelling during the day in the vicinity of LA CLYTTE – LOCRE road. D Coy positions in the valley at M.18.b. chiefly shelled during the afternoon. Several shelters & dug-outs were destroyed. 2/Lt T. Darlington [?] was killed whilst work in progress in digging out the occupants of a dug-out whilst the shelters were in progress. He received the Military Cross for his act of gallantry on July 24.18. D Coy evacuated their position at night & moved back to the SCHERPENBERG LINE. Casualties: 4 OR's killed. 2 OR's wounded.	Batt HQ at M.18.a.6.m.8. & R.G.
	2nd		LA CLYTTE – LOCRE road shelled slightly during the morning & afternoon. At dusk B + D Coys withdrew from the SCHERPENBERG LINE & continued digging a line approximately M/20.2.2 to M.12.b.9.6. which was later termed "THE REDOUBT LINE". The position evacuated by B + D Coys was taken over by a company from the 23rd Middlesex. Casualties: 1 O.R. killed. 4 " wounded.	Lieutenant - Y.O.Res. regimental Batt. Increases - Lieut. Einewerny & other officers Batt.
	3rd		Slight shelling of the LA CLYTTE – LOCRE road & REDOUBT LINE Batt HQs transferred to N.7.C.14 – 23rd Middl. transferred Batt HQs to M.R.682. B+D Coys continued working on new positions throughout the night. Casualties: 2 OR's wounded.	
	4th		2 OR's wounded.	

WAR DIARY of 1/1/9 Batt "The Queens"
INTELLIGENCE SUMMARY. 2.

Army Form C. 2118.

Place	Date 1918	Hour	Summary of Events and Information	Remarks and references to Appendices
Fermoy Sect 28	July 5th		Slight shelling of Support positions. Relieved 23rd Lond. in the front line at night. Reconnaissance patrols sent out. Fourth M.G. in action to his back over support position.	
	6th		Relief completed 1.15am. Slight shelling of FERMOY FARM. Reconnaissance patrols sent out. Patrol damaged M12 crsh shelled during the night. Reorganisation of front line in to 4 section front in squares was formed commenced. Coys working on our position. Casualties 2 ORs wounded.	
	7th		Incurred - 13 other Reported. Batt. from Corner Trees. Slight shelling of front & support positions during the day. Reorganisation of front line completed. Reconnaissance patrols sent out. Fourth M.G. fire again very active on tanks during the night. Coys working on our position at night.	
	8th		Slight shelling of pts N.CRUTTS-LOCRE road, FERMOY FARM & enemy during the day. Patrols sent out at night but did not encounter the enemy. Coys working on our own positions. Casualties - 2/Lt. 6 Puckett & 11 ORs wounded.	
	9th		Incurred - 8 ORs Reported Batt. from Keep, etc. Batt front very quiet during the day. Two patrols sent out at night. One in charge 2/Lt S.Jackson encountered two small parties of the enemy & successfully surprised them. Two kn. wounded 2/Lt Ross reached an enemy post at N.16 c44.35 but found the enemy had evacuated. Coys working on their own position.	
	10th		Slight shelling of support positions during the day. Hostile T.M active on right. Patrols at night. Reconnaissance patrols sent out. Coys working on own positions. Casualties - 3 ORs wounded. Another 1 O.R. from Keep.	

Army Form C. 2118.

WAR DIARY 1/4th Batt "The Queen's"
INTELLIGENCE SUMMARY. 3.

(Erase heading not required.)

Place	Date 1918	Hour	Summary of Events and Information	Remarks and references to Appendices
Ref map Sheet 28.	July 11th		Slight shelling of front line & support positions during the day. The Relief patrols sent out, relieved by 10 O.R. N. rats.	
	12th		Relief by Bats. completed at 2.15am. Batt moved back to reserve position in the WESTOUTRE-GODEWAERT MILL LINE, previously occupied by the 23rd Middx: Batt H.Qrs at M.5.a.13. Remainder of day, resting & cleaning up. Working Parties at night.	Issued 5 O. Returns covering
	13th		Resting & bathing during the day, working parties at night, cable burying & improving WESTOUTRE line.	
	14th		Two coys resting, bathing & cleaning up during the day, one coy working on WESTOUTRE line. Three coys on working parties at night. Batt H.Qrs moved to G.34.d.7. Casualties: 3 O.Rs. wounded. 1 O.R. killed.	
	15th		One coy working during the day. 3 coys working at night on WESTOUTRE line & cable burying. Casualties 1 O.R. killed.	
	16th		One coy working during the day on WESTOUTRE line. 3 coys cable burying at night. Casualties - 4 O.Rs wounded. 1 O.R. wounded.	
	17th		One coy working during the day. 2 coys at night on the WESTOUTRE line. Slight gas shelling during the night in the vicinity of Rabbit hill & the WESTOUTRE line. Coy't J. Furnis & 6 O.Rs went out on covering party between N.13.c.97.40. & N.14.c.43.64. for Engineer raid 2/Lt Jackson & took M.G. fire. The tape was accurately laid in spite of concealment. Casualties: - 1 O.R. killed. 3 O.Rs. wounded. 6 O.Rs. Gassed.	

WAR DIARY of 1/1 Batt. 7th Queens

INTELLIGENCE SUMMARY.

Army Form C. 2118.

Place	Date	Hour	Summary of Events and Information	Remarks and references to Appendices
Ref: Map Sheet 28.	July 1918 18th		One coy working during the day & parts of 3 coys working at night on our positions in the WESTOUTRE line. Ruining hang down (?) Capt Thomas proceeded to assembly positions. Incident – 2 O.Rs. from Coy "A" Wounded. – 3 O.Rs. Wounded.	
	19th		Raid carried out (Point attacked) Garrison & light machine gun captured. One coy working during the day, 3 coys & two Lewis guns working at night on the WESTOUTRE line. Casualties – Capt. J.L. Thomas, Lt. D. Moss, 2/Lt. B. Trotter } Wounded. 4 O.Rs. Killed. 2 O.Rs. missing believed killed. 38 O.Rs.	
	20th		Enemy working during the day. 3 coys working at night. Cable burying. Always bomb raid at 23.30. Mid. in front line.	
	21st		Relief postponed. Enemy patrols encountered in front line. Always enemy on pain our position in WESTOUTRE lines at night. 1 O.R. of the around. Enemy captured with section of 23rd Mid. Casualties – 1 O.R. Accidental. 3 O.Rs Wounded.	
	22nd		Coys resting during the day. Commenced relief of 23rd Mid. in front line at 9.45 p.m.	

Army Form C. 2118.

WAR DIARY of 1st Batt. The Queen's

INTELLIGENCE SUMMARY.

(Erase heading not required.)

Instructions regarding War Diaries and Intelligence Summaries are contained in F. S. Regs., Part II. and the Staff Manual respectively. Title pages will be prepared in manuscript.

Place	Date 1918	Hour	Summary of Events and Information	Remarks and references to Appendices
Re/Maps Sheet 28.	July 22nd		Relief completed at 1.15 a.m. Batt. front very quiet during the day. Our artillery very active during the night in conjunction with a raid by the 122nd Inf. Bde. Slight artillery retaliation on front line & FERMOY FARM. Major E.E. Bowden M.C. killed about 12 noon riding through STEENVOORDE. Casualties - Major E.E. Bowden M.C. & 1 O.R. killed. 1 O.R. wounded.	10 O.Rs from Hospl. &c.
	24th		Slight shelling of support positions during the day. Reconnaissance patrols. Coys working on known positions at night.	
	25th		Slight shelling of A.C.L. 775 - Lockerose during the day. Reconnaissance patrols sent out. Coys working on our positions at night. American General came to reconnoitre front line &c. Increase - 12 O.Rs from Hospl. &c.	
	26th		Batt. front very quiet. Guides sent back at 6 p.m. for American troops. 2 Coys of the 3rd Batt. 106 (U.S) Regt. arrived about 10 p.m. Distributed among the 4th Battalion. R Platoons to each Coy Command for instruction. Surplus British troops (Coys) moved back to N.K.970 T.R. & on Patrols sent out. Intermittent shelling of support positions during the day. Reorganisation of Coys.	
	27th		Slight shell & machine gun fire. American platoons of 3 British Coys working on	

WAR DIARY or INTELLIGENCE SUMMARY

Army Form C. 2118.

Place	Date	Hour	Summary of Events and Information	Remarks and references to Appendices
Ref Map Sheet 28	July 1916 28th (cont)		our positions after consolidation of organization. Reconnaissance patrols sent into enemy's trenches - 4 Officers & 13 O.Rs. entered the enemy's position at 12 Midnight as in report attached. Sniping and shelling throughout day. Troops T.M's active. Very intense from 8 midnight. 10 British carried up relief of front line at 10 p.m. British troops in WESTOUTRE had moved up into support. Patrols sent out.	
	29th		Relief by 10 British completed at 2 am. Enemy troops moved into two coys moved in support positions with the 2 British coys. The WESTOUTRE line. The British troops relieved by Battns moved into their respective coys moved back to positions in the WESTOUTRE line, and occupied by the 5 supply coys. Working parties from all coys at night. Tents are very much cramped. Many sick All coys working on our positions & relief R.Es day & night. Strength = 9 Offrs. reinforcements, 14 O.Rs. from Hospital etc	
	30th		Trench constn, fatigues short stay Personnel sent support from one Battn. between 2 Coys. 2 p.m. reminders of day thirty [?] 2 Officers Coys.	
	31st		Moved up to relieve 9th Rifle Bde in front line at 9pm. 2 Coys in WESTOUTRE line moved back to I.29.c (Shut-27) no opr. 2 coys as support for moved back to billets in this area when relieved by 12th R.Bab Casualties:- 3 O.Rs. Killed, 4 O.Rs. wounded (all Enemy)	

Lanarkshire
[signed] Major

SECRET   Copy No. 3

11th Batt "The Queens" Operation Order No 7 a

Ref: Map Sheet 28 S.W.   5th July 1918.

INTENTION   1. The Battalion will relieve the 23rd Middx Regt in the front line on the night of the 6th/7th inst.

DETAIL   2.(a) 'B' Coy will relieve 'B' Coy of the 23rd Middx on the right of the line.

(b) 'A' Coy will relieve 'A' Coy of the 23rd Middx on the left of the line, with one Platoon in KIMBERLEY TRENCH. This platoon will take over on the night of the 5th/6th July.

(c) 'C' Coy will relieve 'C' Coy of the 23rd Middx in FERMOY FARM Strong Point.

(d) 'D' Coy will relieve 'D' Coy of the 23rd Middx in the line of resistance.

(e) Batt Hqrs will relieve Batt. Hqrs of the 23rd Middx on the LA CLYTTE ROAD.

ADVANCE PARTIES   3. The Coy Commanders of A+B Coys and the 2nd i/c's of C+D Coys with their respective platoon Sergts plus one runner to each officer & Sergt will make a thorough reconnaissance to night 5/6th. The above parties will return to their respective Coys by daylight of morning 6th inst.

MOVEMENT   4. No movement EAST of Batt Hqrs until after dusk.

RATIONS   5. A B & C Coys will draw their rations which will be made up in sandbags (6 rations in a sandbag) BEFORE they move off from their present positions. D Coy will arrange to carry their rations from the dump to A & C Coys previous to relieving D Coy of the 23rd Middx. B Coy will draw their own rations from the dump.

TIME   6. Coys should be able to move at the following times, which are dependant on the quick distribution of rations.

A Coy 11-30 p.m B Coy 12 midnight C Coy 11 p.m D Coy 1-0 a.m.

7. All defence schemes, programmes of work, trench maps & all stores, Coy dumps etc will be handed over on relief. Coy Commanders will ensure that they take over all information regarding enemy movement, ours & enemy patrols, enemy positions etc

8. Completion of relief will be reported to Batt Hqrs by runner as quickly as possible.

9. Acknowledge.

                                         (Sgd) C. H. BROMHEAD
                                              2/Lt A/Adjt

Issued by runner at
Copy No			
1	C.O.	9	Signalling Offr
2	2nd i/c	10	Transport
3	Adjt	11	Medical
4	123 Bgde	12	R S M
5	A Coy	13	Quartermaster
6	B	14	File
7	C	15	War Diary
8	D	16	23rd Middx

SECRET.   Copy No.........

INSTRUCTIONS No.7B.

MAP REFERENCE Sheet 28 S.W.

ACTION IN CASE OF ATTACK. (See INSTRUCTIONS No.7A.).

1. (a) The two front line companies will offer the most determined resistance. They will only be withdrawn by direct orders from Battn.H.Q. and only then if overwhelmed by a greatly superior force of infantry.
   If compelled to withdraw, they will fight every yard of the ground back to their next positions.
   (b) The Left Front Coy. will, if the above situation arises, be withdrawn to the FERMOY FARM Strong Point, the Right Front Coy. to a line on the forward slope of DEVON CAMP Locality.
   The above withdrawals would be covered by the fire of every rifle and Lewis Gun that can be brought to bear and supported by Machine Guns and Trench Mortars, particularly by the cross fire from the FERMOY FARM and KIMBERLEY TRENCH Positions.
   (c) The FERMOY FARM and KIMBERLEY TRENCH Positions will be held to the last in order to break up an attack on the Main Line of Resistance and especially to frustrate any attack up the SCHERPENBERG - PAN DON VALLEY, by cross fire.
   (d) The Company holding the Right of the Line of Resistance will hold on at all costs.

2. **COUNTER ATTACKS. (See INSTRUCTIONS No.7A.).**

   (a) Coy.Commanders will forthwith prepare in writing, orders for their counter attack platoons.
   (b) It must be remembered that to achieve the most decisive results, a counter attack must be delivered quickly against the flanks of a break through and not against the head.
   (c) All Officers and N.C.O's will reconnoitre the ground over which they may have to counter attack.
   (d) The Counter Attack Company in FERMOY FARM will only move on orders from Battn.H.Q. unless as otherwise laid down in INSTRUCTIONS No.7A. It will be prepared to counter attack in the following eventualities of a break through at :-

          I.   FAIRY HOUSE.
         II.   BUTTERFLY FARM.
        III.   GARDEN FARM. "A" or "B".
        IV.   PAN DON.

   In the event of I, after a counter attack has been made, the Coy. would probably have to take up a defensive flank to the Brigade Front to the Right.
   The same orders apply to III. If a break through was made near the LA CLYTTE - KEMMEL ROAD, after the counter attack, a defensive flank to the Brigade Front would have to be formed to the Left. The ground will therefore be reconnoitred with the above possibilities in view.
   (e) All such counter attacks will be supported by machine guns and trench mortars.
   Platoon Commanders will neglect no opportunity of supporting such counter attacks as may take place with rifle and Lewis Gun fire.
   (f) All ranks must be made acquainted with Counter Attack Schemes. Much depends on this and units cannot possibly move quickly with success unless all ranks know previously what is expected from them. All Officers and other ranks must fully understand that counter attack troops are quite distinct from the garrison of a trench, yet accommodation may be such that they both have to live in the same trench.

/ At the

At the same time, counter attack troops may quite likely be called upon to defend their position, particularly if the enemy are on top of them before a counter attack is possible. Therefore positions occupied by counter attack troops must be made defendable regarding firesteps, Lewis Gun positions and wire etc.

W.Owen
Lieut.Colonel.
Commanding 11th Bn. "The Queen's"(R.W.S.)Regt.

July 10th 1918.

Issued by runner at ....

```
Copy No.1. - C.O.
  "   "  2. - 123rd Inf.Bde.
  "   "  3. - O.C. "A" Coy.
  "   "  4. - O.C. "B"  "
  "   "  5. - O.C. "C"  "
  "   "  6. - O.C. "D"  "
  "   "  7. - War Diary.
  "   "  8. - File.
```

SECRET   COPY NO 3.

11th Batt "The Queens" Operation Order No 8.

Ref Map Sheet 28 SW.   10th July 1918

INTENTION 1. The Battalion will be relieved by the 10th R.W Kents in the front line on the night of the 11th/12th inst.
On completion of relief the Battn will move into the reserve area at KASTEEL MILL, at present occupied by the 23rd Middx.

DETAIL 2.
a. 'D' Coy of the 10th Kents will relieve 'A' on the left of the line.
b. 'B' Coy of the 10th Kents will relieve 'B' Coy on the right of the line.
c. 'A' Coy of the 10th Kents will relieve 'C' Coy at FERMOY FARM strong point.
d. 'C' Coy of the 10th Kents will relieve 'D' Coy on the right of the line of resistance.
e. Batt. Hqrs of the 10th Kents will relieve Batt Hqrs on the LA CLYTTE ROAD.

ADVANCE PARTIES 3.
a. One guide per section from the six front line platoons, & 1 NCO per platoon throughout the Battn, & 1 guide per Coy Hqrs will report at Batt Hqrs at 1-0AM 11th inst. They will later report to their opposite numbers of the 10th Kents, remain with them, & will guide their respective units to the line to-morrow night, conforming with all orders of the 10th Kents.
b. Corresponding advance parties with the addition of one Offr per Coy Hqrs from the 10th Kents will report to each Coy Hqrs to-night. They will live with their opposite numbers during the day 11th inst. They will meet their respective Coy guides at Batt Hqrs at 10 p.m tonight.
c. The 10th Kents will arrive on the night of 11th/12th by platoons. Section guides will meet their sections at platoon Hqrs, & platoon NCO guides will meet their platoons at Coy Hqrs. One Offr from C Coy 10th Kents will report to O.C D Coy & take over all work on hand.

(2)

(d) One NCO per platoon, & one NCO from Batt Hqrs will report at Batt Hqrs at 1-30 am 11th inst. They will proceed to the reserve area, & take over from their opposite numbers of the 23rd Middx. Senior NCO per Coy will also take over respective Coy Hqrs. The above NCO's will meet their platoons at road junction M.12.a.1.4. to-morrow night 11th inst.

MOVEMENT 4. No movement EAST of reserve Batt. area is to take place until after dusk.

RATIONS 5. Rations are being dumped in the reserve area at KASTEEL MILL.

6. One L.G. limber per Coy will be at the ration dump M.12.a.7.6 at 11 pm. Two limbers will report at Batt. Hqrs after dumping rations at KASTEEL MILL.

7. No petrol tins will be handed over, all empty tins will be carried out.

8. All defence schemes, programmes of work, Trench maps and stores, information obtained by patrols etc etc, will be handed over on relief.
All front line sections, & all other platoons, will form dumps, shovels & ammunition etc. These will be handed over on relief, & receipts obtained.

9. Completion of relief will be reported by wire as follows:—

   A Coy — HOW
   B Coy — IS
   C Coy — YOUR
   D Coy — FATHER

10. Batt. Hqrs will close here on completion of relief, & open at KASTEEL MILL at same hour.

11. Acknowledge.

(Sgd) C.H. BROMHEAD
2 Lt a/adjt

Issued by runner at
Copy No 1 C.O.
2 2 i/c
3 adjt
4 173 Bgde
5 A Coy
6 B Coy
7 C Coy
8 D Coy
9 Lg Off
10 Transpt
11 M.Med
12 R.S.M.
13 Quartermaster
14 File
15 War Diary
16 R.W. Kents

S.E./R.M.T.   Copy No. 7.

11th Bn. "The Queen's" (R.W.S.) Regiment.
OPERATION ORDER No. 2.

Ref.Map 28 S.W.1.   16th July 1918.

INTENTION.   1. (a) A Raid will be made by the Battalion on the enemy
                      position opposite left of the Front Line, Centre
                      Sector, on the night of the   July 1918.

                  (b) To capture prisoners and to do as much damage as
                      possible to the enemy in personnel and material.

OBJECTIVES.   2.   Enemy First, Second, and Third Line defensive
                     positions between a line running through N 13 d 96.40
                     and N 20 a 27.90, and a line running through
                     N 14 c 72.13 and N 14 c 43.67.

TASK ALLOT-   3. (a) The frontage is allotted as follows :-
MENT.   From the right boundary to the track running through
                      N 14 c inclusive:-
                          One Platoon "D" Coy. plus 1 Lewis Gun Section.

                  (b) From above track exclusive to Left boundary:-
                          One Platoon "A" Coy. plus 1 Lewis Gun Section.

ASSEMBLY   4.   The Assembly Position will be marked out by a tape
POSITION.   or wire on a line running from N 13 d 97.40 to
                     N 14 c 43.67.
                     O.C. RAID will place this tape or wire in position
                     with direction tapes for each Section, on the
                     previous night.
                     On the night of the Raid, Parties will move up by
                     the PUMP LANE - GARDEN FARM "A" Track, and will be
                     in position at least half an hour previous to
                     ZERO Hour.

THE ADVANCE. 5. I. From position of assembly, Parties will proceed
                     across No Man's Land in two waves.
                  (a) Each Platoon - less one Section - in a line of
                      sections in file at approximately an equal interval
                      to fill the frontage.

                  (b) One Section per Platoon in extended order, (men in
                      three's) covering the whole frontage in rear of (a)
                      to mop up and give support where necessary.

                  (c) One Lewis Gun Team per Platoon will cover the advance
                      by engaging enemy machine guns or enemy troops
                      endeavouring to get in rear of Parties, the right
                      gun paying particular attention to enemy post at
                      N 14 c 95.12. They will keep within 30 to 60 yds.
                      of the rear of the "moppers up" and will cover the
                      withdrawal.

                  II.(a) ZERO plus ½ minute - Advance to First Line of Posts.
                         (As far as possible the advance will commence as
                         the barrage comes down).

                  (b) ZERO plus 5 minutes - Advance to Second Line of
                      Posts.

                  (c) ZERO plus 8 minutes - Advance to Third Line of
                      Posts.

- 2 -

(d) Withdrawal will commence at ZERO plus 15 minutes or before, and should be complete by ZERO plus 30 minutes.
For phases of operations see Appendix I.

ARMS and EQUIPMENT. 6. See Appendix II.

ACTION OF ARTILLERY. 7. Details to follow.
SUMMARY OF ARTILLERY ACTION:- Artillery Barrage will be brought down somewhat in the form of A Box-Barrage. The minimum inside safety limits for the Box-Barrage being N 13 d 96.40., N 20 a 22.90., N 14 c 72.15., N 14 c 43.67.
All enemy positions, machine guns, &c. outside this 'box' likely to be troublesome will be dealt with by Howitzers and 18-pdrs from ZERO to ZERO plus 25 minutes, the only exceptions to the above being as follows:-
At ZERO the artillery will drop the far side of the 'box' on to the enemy 2nd and 3rd Lines of Posts (within the 'box').
At ZERO plus 3 minutes the barrage will lift about 70 yards, clearing the 2nd Line of Enemy Posts between N 14 c 15.10. and N 14 c 65.35.
At ZERO plus 5 minutes the barrage will lift clear of the area to be raided.

TRENCH MORTARS. 8. Details to follow.
SUMMARY OF T.M.ACTION:- Five Stokes Mortars will be in position in the Trench Cutting the track at N 13 d 60.57. at ZERO minus at least 1 hour.
The positions will be dug and ammunition dumped in position on the night previous to the Raid.
At Zero plus 0 to Zero plus 1, an intense fire from the four guns will be brought to bear on the First Line of Enemy Posts, pin-points to be given later.
From ZERO plus 0 to ZERO plus 5, one T.M. will engage enemy machine gun post at N 14 c No. 12.
Trench Mortars will remain in action prepared to give covering fire to the withdrawal of the Raiding Parties, but will not fire unless the position is clear.

Cancelled

MACHINE GUNS. 9. Details to follow.
SUMMARY OF MACHINE GUN ACTION:- Machine Guns will engage targets actively in conjunction with the Artillery 'box' safety limits, paying particular attention to the enemy machine guns on the forward slopes of MT.KEMMEL and known enemy machine guns on the remainder of the enemy front line (Centre Sector).

COMMUNICATIONS and SIGNALS. 10. The Battalion Signalling Officer will make all necessary arrangements. A wire will be run out to a point in the Front Line Trenches to be known as "O.C. RAID Forward H.Q." approximately N 14 c 20.75. This will be connected up with a line running to old Company H.Q. SNOBWOOD approximately N 13 a 20.30. to be known as "O.C. RAID Rear H.Q.".

CODE. 11. The following Code Words will be used in connection with this Operation:-
TROUT. - Operation postponed for 60 minutes.
SALMON. - Operation cancelled for the day.
SHRIMPS. - Cease fire.
WHALES. - All doing well.
MUSSELS. - Resistance.
CRABS. - Prisoners returning.

/ MINNOWS.

- 3 -

                MINUTES.- Casualties.
                PIKE.   - Party returning.
                COD.   - All in.

COLLECTING STATION.   12.   All Raiders' prisoners, captured documents, and material will be sent to O.C. RAID Rear H.Q. From here prisoners, booty &c. will be sent to Forward Brigade H.Q. and handed over.

MEDICAL.   13.   An Advanced Aid Post will be established in the Advanced POMPIER TRENCH leading off the PUMP LANE GARDEN FARM "A" CAMP TRACK. From here all casualties will be taken to AID POST at O.C.RAID Rear H.Q., thence to R.A.P. in the LA CLYTTE - LOCRE ROAD.

SYNCHRONIZATION.   14.   Watches will be synchronised at Brigade H.Q. by all concerned at ZERO minus 6 hours.
The Signalling Officer will attend.

REPORTS.   15.   All reports to O.C. RAID Rear H.Q.

                ACKNOWLEDGE.

                                    (Sgd) W.L. Owen.

                                          Lieut.Colonel.
Commanding 11th Bn. "The Queen's" Regiment.

Issued by Runner at 10 p.m. 16th July 1918.

                Copy No. 1. - O.C. RAID.
                "   " 2. - C. O.
                "   " 3)
                "   " 4) - 123rd Inf.Bde.
                "   " 5. - 123rd L.T.M.Bty.
                "   " 6. - 41st Bn.M.G.C.
                "   " 7. - File.
                "   " 8. - War Diary.
                "   " 9. - Spare.

S E C R E T.   Copy No...7..

AMENDMENT TO OPERATION ORDER No.9. DATED 16-7-18.

17th July 1918.

Para 5, sub-para II, sub-para (a).

ZERO plus 1 minute will read ZERO plus 0 minutes.

Para. 8.

Trench Mortars cancelled.

APPENDIX II, Para.3. "AMMUNITION".

2 bombs per man, "moppers up" only.

W.C. Owen
Lieut.Colonel.
Commanding 11th Bn."The Queen's" Regt.

Issued by runner at   m.
Issued to all recipients of Operation Order No.9. dated 16-7-18.

SECRET. Copy No. 7...

ADDENDA

AMENDMENT TO OPERATION ORDER No.9. DATED 16-7-18.

17th July 1918.

In the event of the barrage being required for a further 15 minutes a French Very Light bursting into 4 stars will be sent up by O.C. RAID from the front line.

Headquarters and C.O. of the 11th Queen's and all Liaison Officers will be at Divisional O.P. on the left of the Line of Resistance, Centre Sector.

W C Owen
Lieut. Colonel.
Commanding 11th Bn. "The Queen's" Regiment.

Issued by runner at   m.
Issued to all recipients of Operation Order No.9. dated 16-7-18.

REPORT ON RAID.
Carried out by the 11th Queen's Regt.
On Night of 18th/19th July, 1918.

The night was extremely light until about midnight, and this, though interfering slightly with the Assembly, in that the parties were observed and fired upon by machine guns when taking up their positions, did not prevent the Assembly being complete at 11.55 p.m.

During the following 35 minutes two O.K. messages were received by me from O.C. RAID.

At 1.27½ a.m. several guns of the barrage opened fire. At 1.29 a.m. the machine guns opened fire; the whole gradually intensifying until at 1.30 a.m. all arms taking part in the barrage were firing; the ultimate issue of this being that the line did not jump forward from the Assembly Tape as simultaneously as was intended.

The Right Platoon, commanded and gallantly led by Lieut. Britt Trotter left the tape at Zero and went forward with great dash right up to the forward shell hole posts. Lieut. Trotter was slightly to the left of the posts, but the enemy held up the Section opposite the post with a machine gun at very close range.

Lieut. Trotter grasped the situation immediately, ordered a burst of fire from his men, and followed it up with a charge.

Out of the seven or eight of the enemy manning the parapet of this consolidated shell hole, one was shot through the head with the burst of rifle fire, three were bayoneted and killed, and three were taken prisoners.

The enemy here put up a fight, most determined though of short duration, and as soon as the charge took place most of them left their parapet. Two attacked Lieut. Trotter with the bayonet. Cpl. Finlayson got in first and bayoneted them both. The remainder then dived into their dugouts which were constructed in a trench connecting up two shell holes, covered over with corrugated iron sheeting and camouflaged.

One of the enemy had to be "picked" out of his shelter on the bayonet before the three remaining surrendered. When asked why they did not surrender at once they replied, "English no take prisoners".

At this stage Lieut. Trotter had lost several men, and had just received a bad wound in the shoulder. He, however, got his men on the move towards the next enemy position. Before reaching it, he became stupified and apparently fainted.

Recovering, he pushed forward and threw the enemy wire, which was really no obstacle, being a few strands only plus a trip-wire.

A considerable amount of execution was done in this trench, though most of the trench was covered over with corrugated sheeting, forming fairly secure shelters.

Then Cpl. Larkins with his Lewis Gun followed Lieut. Trotter's Platoon and considerably helped with fire to the Right, keeping the enemy's heads down. In fact, previous to ZERO he engaged a machine gun firing from the Right, and later silenced it.

Cpl. Finlayson's inspiring example and fine fighting qualities materially helped towards the success of this Platoon. He brought in three prisoners, and an enemy medium machine gun.

L/Cpl. Nicholls captured the gun in magnificent style.

Pte Bullen, stretcher bearer, carried Lieut. Trotter in after he again became unconscious. His work was highly satisfactory and courageous throughout.

The casualties of this Platoon were 1 officer and 15 Other Ranks Wounded, 1 Other Rank killed, and two Other Ranks Missing; believed Killed.

Though the majority of these were caused by enemy machine guns, rifles, and trench mortars, a percentage were from our own shells. The "box" appeared to be too close in on the Right.

/The Left

The Left Platoon was most courageously led and commanded by Lieut. Moon. He left the tape almost as soon as the first few shells of the barrage came down.

An enemy machine gun opened from the direction of KIM CAMP. This was silenced by Cpl. Sandells by very clever and active manipulation of his gun.

It was not expected that this party would meet with opposition until reaching the enemy 2nd Line. This was so, except for the activity of the machine gun referred to.

About the line of the shell holes three men were seen running back towards their line. Lieut. Moon dashed forward, bayoneted two, and sent the third back as a prisoner, wounded.

Identifications were collected in a sandbag, and a light machine gun extracted from a shell hole; all being, however, ultimately lost. It is supposed a shell put the party out of action.

On the Left the Bosche was seen to be running away, and going through a gap in his wire. Cpl. Sandells, now wounded in the leg, brought fire to bear on this gap, and was satisfied that he and his gun did great execution here.

Lieut. Moon was greatly pleased by the excellent line that his whole platoon kept. They arrived in their respective parties with practically their correct intervals up against this double belt of concertina wire quite hidden from view in the high corn.

The wire was being cut all along the line and our men were gradually getting through. The whole Platoon, however, suffered so seriously from our barrage, Lieut. Moon himself being hit on three separate occasions, that further progress became impossible, and the Platoon withdrew. The whole party arrived back between 1.55 a.m. and 2.0 a.m.

Cpl. Sandells, though wounded, returned with his gun.

Sgt. Walsh, who was in charge of the "moppers up", filled a gap at the last moment, and by his capable leadership rendered invaluable assistance to Lieut. Moon, and though badly wounded did not give in.

Pte Webb carried Lieut. Moon on his back right from the enemy wire to our front line. His work throughout was very fine.

The casualties of this Platoon were 1 Officer and 23 Other Ranks wounded, and 2 Other Ranks Missing, believed Killed.

GENERAL SUMMARY.

The Artillery Barrage was good, but improperly timed. The Machine Guns firing from the left of the Divisional O.P. were weak, (possibly due to the enemy barrage).

The enemy replied actively within 3 minutes with a light trench mortar barrage practically along the Sunken Road through GARDEN FARM "B" CAMP. The principal barrage fell on FERMOY FARM and forward of the left of the SCHERPENBERG - DICKEBUSCH LAKE Line, lengthening out about 10 minutes afterwards to the latter line.

The barrage was not heavy, but in the front the impression was that it fell in depth.

The general alertness of the enemy was probably due to the relief having just taken place.

The Assembly Tape proved a great success; also the rehearsal of the Assembly Positions with the various party leaders during the previous night.

The three officers concerned laid great stress on the utility of both the above.

The parties, followed by the "moppers up", gave great satisfaction.

On the whole, the going in NO MAN'S LAND was comparatively good; the condition of the ground was not a serious obstacle to good progress.

Capt. Furness considered that a great number of the enemy were killed, and estimates the minimum at 30.

Capt. Furness was wounded at 1.55 a.m.

/Lieut Jackson

Lieut. Jackson rendered great assistance throughout. Whilst the Assembly Tape was being put out on the previous evening he patrolled forward of it. He also carried on afterwards until daylight. He remained in the line all day guarding the Assembly Position, and was out again with his party on the evening of the Raid; again guarding the tape. During the raid apart from rendering valuable assistance to Capt. Furness in and around our wire, it was largely due to his efforts that the wounded were got in and away. He passed unconcernedly through the enemy barrage three times.

The enemy barrage had quietened down at 2.5 a.m.

The quantity and variety of coloured lights was amazing. They were double and single red, green, white and gold; and golden rain breaking into about 7, and white parachute lights floating along the front. At 2.10 a.m. 14 green stars went up from the Right of KEMMEL, whilst on the left 13 similar ones were observed.

The work of the Stretcher Bearers under Cpl. Hazell was highly creditable. He and his men worked under trying conditions, causing general admiration.

The assistance rendered by the 23rd Middx. Regt., and particularly by Pte Briggs, stretcher bearer of "A" Coy., of the Middx. Regt., as well as by parties from the 20th Durham L.I. was beyond praise. The latter, by their ready assistance, enabled casualties to be evacuated, which otherwise would have been impossible until the following night.

Capt. Furness was magnificent throughout. He inspired his officers and men to great efforts.

The leadership of the Section Leaders was of a very high order. All ranks went forward with great determination, and returned in high spirits, (though many of them were wounded) feeling that they had given the Hun a bad time.

Lieut. Colonel.
Commanding 11th Bn. "The Queen's" Regt.

19th July 1918.

SECRET.   Copy No ___

1st Bn The Queen's Operation Order No 10

Ref Map. Sheet 28 S.W. 1/10000
                                                            20th July 18.

INTENTION 1. The battalion will relieve the 23rd Middlesex
              in the front line on the night of the 21/22 inst.

DETAIL   2. B Coy 1st Queens will relieve C. Coy 23rd Midd. Right Front.
              D   "   "   "   "   "   "   D   "   "   "   Left Front.
              C   "   "   "   "   "   "   B   "   "   "   FERMOY FARM.
              A   "   "   "   "   "   "   A   "   "   "   Support.

ADVANCE   3 (a) 1 N.C.O. per platoon, & 1 N.C.O. per Coy H Qs
PARTIES   & 1 N.C.O. from Batt HQs of the 23rd Midd.
                will report tomorrow morning (21st inst) at 10 a.m.
                to Batt HQs. They will later report to
                the Coy HQs of their opposite numbers,
                remain with them, & will guide their
                respective units to the line tomorrow night.

           (b) 1 guide per section from the front line the
                platoons of B & D Coys except Lewis Gun teams
                & front line, 1 N.C.O. from all remaining
                platoons throughout the battalion, 1 guide also
                per Coy HQs & 1 NCO from Batt HQs
                will report at 1 a.m. tonight 20/21st to Batt
                HQs of the 23rd Midd: M 17 c 8 2. They
                will later proceed to their opposite
                numbers in the line & take over duties of
                work, defence schemes (except Batt Defence
                Scheme) air photos, trench maps, &
                information from patrols etc.
                The above party will take one day's
                rations.

                Section guides will wait for their platoons
                at Plat HQs on the night of the 21st & will

(c) 1 officer per coy & 1 NCO per platoon from the 2 front line coys & the coy in the FERMOY FARM strong point of the 23rd Mid. will remain in the line with their appointed runners, 24 hours after relief.

(d) officers from the 23rd Mid will report to Bn HQ at 10 a.m. 21st & take over all details of work

MOVEMENT 4. No movement of the above batt: is to take place until after dusk.

RATIONS 5. Two days rations will be issued on the night 20/21st.

6. Two limbers will report to Batt Hqs at 11 p.m. tomorrow night. Coy mess boxes & officers kit valises, will be dumped at the side of the road by C Coy HQs, & will be taken by these limbers to Batt HQ in Le Cleytte Road.

7. ——————— over.

8. All defence schemes, programmes of work, Trench maps & others will be handed over & a receipt obtained.

9. Completion of relief will be reported by wiring the code word "COWAN".

10. Batt HQ will close here at 9 pm & open at the same time at M12c88.

11. Acknowledge.

Issued by runners at

Copy No					
1	CO	8	C Coy	12	RSM
2	2/C	8	D Coy	13	Lt QM
	Adj	9	SC	14	23 Mid
	123 Bde	10	T.O	15	File
	A Coy	11	M.O		

To O/C. Adjt.   O/O/137

Addendum to O/O No 10

Coys will move off in the following
order by platoons at 100ˣ intervals
  B . D . C . A
Time for the 1st platoon of B Coy to
move off at ~~dusk~~ will to be left to the
discretion of the Coy Commander

    (Sgd) C. H. BROMHEAD
     2/Lt A/Adjt.
21.7.18   DONV.

To Adjt   Copy No. 3
                                                          21st July 1918.

AMENDMENTS TO O.O. No 10

(1) For the night 21/22nd read the night 22/23rd.

(2) Para 3(a) is cancelled. The middle guides will report at 9-30 am to-morrow morning 22nd to B.H.Q. Later they will proceed to the reserve area of the 124th Bgde.

      Para 3(b) is cancelled. Advance party will return to-night 21/22nd, to their respective units & guide them into the line on the night 22/23rd.

(3) Para 7 Add "as many petrol cans as possible will be sent to Batt H Qrs".

(4) Acknowledge

                                             (Sgd) C.H. BROMHEAD
                                                2/Lt A/Adjt "DoWu"

Issued to all recipients of O/O's dated 21st

SECRET.   Copy No. 2.

11th Batt. "The Queens" Operation Order No 11.

Ref. Map. Sheet 28 S.W.   July 25th 1918

INTENTION. 1. Two Coys of the 106th American Infantry Regt will be attached to the Battalion for instruction on the night 26/27th. They will be distributed throughout the area at present occupied by the Battn. On completion of the distribution, A & C Coys less Coy HQrs complete, will withdraw to the WESTOUTRE - GOED MOET MILL LINE under the 2nd i/c of each company.

DETAIL OF DISTRIBUTION & RELIEF

(2) a. Nos 1 & 2 American platoons (M Coy) will be attached to O.C. 'D' Coy, & Nos 3 & 4 American platoons (I Coy) will be attached to O.C. 'B' Coy.

(b) Two sections of these platoons will be attached to each platoon of D & B Coys, & will be distributed amongst the 4 sections in each case.

(c) One British section from the right & left platoons of D & B Coy respectively will then be sent back to their respective counter-attack platoon positions & the two present counter-attack platoons will then withdraw, in the case of D Coy, to the SCHERPENBERG - DICKEBUSCH LAKE LINE & in the case of B Coy, to the FERMOY FARM strong point. D Coy platoon commander will report arrival to O.C. 'A' Coy, & B Coy platoon commander will report to O.C. 'C' Coy.

(d) Two more British sections from the left & right platoons of D & B Coys will be sent to the centre platoons. These two sections will be distributed between the four posts & the present centre platoons will withdraw & report arrival as detailed in para C above.

(e) The result of this relief & distribution will be that all posts in D & B Coys will consist of half British troops & half American troops & each platoon under the command of O.C. 'D' & 'B' Coys

(2)

will actually consist of – though mixed – 2 British sections & 2 American sections.

(3) a. Nos 5 & 6 American platoons (M Coy) & nos 7 & 8 American platoons (I Coy) will report to C & A Coys respectively in addition to the two platoons from D & B respectively. When all of these platoons have reported, C & A Coys less their Coy HQrs will proceed under 2nd i/c's to the WESTOUTRE GOED MOET MILL LINE.

(b) The result of this relief will leave O.C 'C' Coy in command of two platoons of 'B' Coy & 2 American platoons, & O.C 'A' Coy in command of 2 platoons of 'D' Coy & 2 American platoons. These two commands will be reorganized so that all sections consist of half British & half American troops.

(c) C & A Coys will leave one NCO per platoon in their present positions for 24 hrs after relief.

GUIDES (4) a. Four guides from each Coy will report to 2/Lt Conway to-night (25th), & remain at B.H.Q & guide the American platoons to their respective Coys in the line to-morrow night.

(b) Four guides, including 1 NCO each, from C & A Coy will report to Lt Cowan to-night (25th) – later they will reconnoitre their prospective positions in the WESTOUTRE GOET MOET MILL LINE & guide their respective platoons out of the line after relief on the night 26/27th.

All guides should wait for their rations before reporting.

'A' Coy guides will report & return to their Coy & wait instructions.

(c) One guide per platoon from D & B Coys will wait at their respective Coy HQrs on the night 26/27th, & guide the American sections to platoon HQrs. One guide per section from the six front line platoons of D & B Coys will wait at their respective

(3)

platoon HQrs on the night 26/27th, & guide American personnel to their sections.

(5) a. O.C. 'D' Coy will arrange for the reconnaissance of the positions in SCHERPENBERG LINE & also the best route back from the present positions.

(b). O.C. 'B' Coy will arrange for the reconnaissance of the FERMOY FARM strong point & routes.

RATIONS (6) a. Rations for C & A Coys less Coy HQrs will be dumped at the WESTOUTRE LINE. Position of dump to be notified later.

b. Rations for the 4 platoons of D & B Coys remaining in the front line will be made up in bundles of threes.

Rations for the remaining 4 platoons of D & B Coys will be sent to the SCHERPENBERG LINE & FERMOY FARM respectively.

c. Rations for all Coy HQrs will be as usual.

(7) Completion of the relief & distribution will be reported to this office by using the code word "CHITTY".

(8) Acknowledge.

[signature]
2Lt a/Adjt
for O.C. 11th "Queens" (R.W.S.)

Issued to signals at

Copy no 1 C.O   Copy no 6 C Coy
    " 2 Adjt   " 7 D "
    " 3 123 Inf. Bde   " 8 Lt & Qrmstr
    " 4 A Coy   " 9 107th U.S.A. Inf. Regt
    " 5 B "   " 10 War Diary

To 2nd Lt G. Conway.

Ref Operation Order No 11 dated July 25th/18

(1) 4 guides per company are reporting to you to night 25/26. They will bring their rations & remain at Batt H Qrs. (in the case of A Coy, they can return to their Coy & wait instructions) Tomorrow they will proceed with you to the cross roads at G 32 c 2 2 (Sheet 28 1/40,000).

You should arrive with your party at this point at 8pm when you will wait for the 2 coys of the 106th American Infantry Regt (M & I coys)

(2) You will be responsible that these coys proceed from this point in half platoons & that each half platoon has it correct guide who will guide their two 1/2 platoons to their respective Coy HQs.

(3) These guides must be shewn the route they are to pursue & you will be responsible that they do not proceed E of KASTEEL Mill by the road until it is sufficiently dark. P.T.O

(4) You will ~~at~~ be responsible that, an interval of at least 100ˣ is kept between half platoons.

(5)

C Birkenhead
2/Lt a/Adj
for O.C. 1st Queens.

Regarding Para 3. Owing to ~~only~~ there only being 4½ hours of darkness now, it is essential that no effort should be spared to get the American troops up here as quickly as possible. With this in view, the ~~so~~ vicinity of Kastell Mill should be reconnoitred for a covered route ~~to~~ ~~with to~~ permit movement past ~~of~~ KASTEEL MILL before dark.

TABLE FOR GUIDES

First two American platoons (only) Nos 1 & 2 D Coy Left Front.
~~Second~~ " " " Nos 3 & 4 (I Coy) B Coy Right "
Third " " " Nos 5 & 6 (II Coy) C Coy FERMOY FARM
~~Fourth~~ " " " Nos 7 & 8 (I Coy) A Coy Saifo part

7. (a) No petrol cans will be handed over. The cans containing tomorrow's (20th) tea will be sent to Batt HQ as ~~soon~~ when emptied tomorrow. ~~The two limbers with~~ The R.S.M. will arrange for someone to be left in charge of these & the limbers will pick them up on their return from the BtN Qr LACLYTTE road.

(b) The R.S.M. will arrange to supply all coys with water as soon after relief as possible.

SECRET.   Copy No. 1

11th Batt: The Queens' Operation Order No 13

Ref: Map Sheet 28 S.W.1.   July 27th 1918

INTENTION 1. The Battn & American personnel less
the details of C & A Coys in the
WESTOUTRE LINE will be relieved by the
10th R.W. Kents on the night of the 28/29th inst. On
completion of relief the Battn & American personnel
will occupy the support positions at present
occupied by the 10th R.W. Kents.

DETAILS 2(a) Left Front Coy will be relieved by A Coy 10th Kents
            Right   "   "   "   "   "   C   "   "
            FERMOY (FARM) "   "   "   B   "   "
            Support   "   "   "   D   "   "

(b) At dusk the details of C & A Coys will
relieve B & C Coys of the 10th R.W. Kents respectively
in support.
The two American platoons (I Coy) at present
under the command of OC A Coy & No 13 platoon
D Coy will relieve A Coy of the 10th R.W. Kents
in support.

(c) The two American platoons (I Coy) at present
under the command of OC B Coy, when
relieved, will pick up guides here, & proceed
to the positions at present occupied by A Coy
of the 10th R.W. Kents.

(d) The American platoons of A Coy when relieved

(2)

will pick up guides here & proceed to the positions at present occupied by D Coy 10th R.W.K.

(e) The remaining platoons of D Coy, & the platoons of B Coy, when relieved, will proceed to the positions at present occupied by A & C Coys respectively in the WESTOUTRE LINE.

(f) On completion of all reliefs, Coy Commanders (including American personnel) will assume their normal commands.

ADVANCE PARTIES 3. (a) One NCO per American platoon, one NCO per platoon from A & C Coys, & one NCO from the B platoon will report here at 12 midnight tonight 27/28th inst. Later, they will proceed to the Coy HQrs of their opposite numbers of the 10th Kents, take over the positions & remain there until their respective units arrive on the night 28/29th.

(b) A corresponding numbers of guides from the 10th R.W.K. will report here at 8 pm on the night of the 28/29th, & later guide their opposite numbers of this unit to their respective positions in support.

(c) One NCO per the 3 remaining platoons of D Coy & one NCO per platoon from B Coy will report here at 12 midnight. Later they will report to O.C. A & C Coys details in the WESTOUTRE LINE, remain there & take over positions, meet their respective platoons at M.T.2 d.1.4. to-morrow night 28/29th & guide them back.

ATTACHMENTS 4. In addition to the attachment laid down in O.O. No 12, on completion of relief, the 2nd i/c of

(3)

B Coy will be attached to I Coy (American) &
2nd i/c of D Coy will be attached to M Coy (American)

5(a) All defence schemes (except Brigade Defence scheme)
programmes of work, trench maps & stores,
information obtained by patrols etc., will be handed
over on relief. Receipts will be obtained & a
duplicate forwarded to this office by 2pm on the
29th inst.

(b) Seconds in command of Coys will arrange to take
over stores etc from opposite numbers of the 10th RWK
tomorrow 28th inst.

RATIONS 6(a) Rations will be dumped at the Batt dump.
Details of ration parties will be notified later.
(b) No petrol cans will be handed over.

7. Completion of relief will be reported by wiring
the code word NEWMAN

8 Batt HQrs will close here on completion of
relief & open at same time at support HQrs M12 d 72

9 Acknowledge.

(Sgd) C H BROMHEAD
2Lt A/Adjt
HORN.

Issued to Signals at

Copy no 1 Co	Copy no 6 C Coy	Copy no 12 I O 50 + 69 C
2 Adj	7 D	13 OC 4th C Amm
3 173 Bgde	8 Adj 3rd B. USA Ryl	14 MO
4 A Coy	9 11 Qms	15 War Diary
5 B	10 10 RWK	16 FILE
	11 RSM	

SECRET   Copy No 2.

11th Batt "The Queens" Operation Order No 12

Ref Map 11net 28.S.W. 1/10000   July 27th 1918

INTENTION 1. Reorganisation of British & American Troops

DETAIL 2 (a) O's C Coys will reorganise their present Coys into two platoons of British Troops & two platoons of American Troops.

(b) O's C the two front line companies will arrange to have, on completion of this reorganisation, their two flank platoons British, & their centre & counter attack platoons American.

(c) One Senior British NCO is to be attached to each American platoon on completion of the reorganisation, and one Lewis Gun number to each American L G Team.

REPORTS 3. Completion of relief to be wired to this office by using the code word CONWAY

4. Acknowledge

                            [signature]
                            2/Lt a/Adjt
                            HQRS

Issued by runners at
- Copy No 1 C.O
- 2 Adjt
- 3 183 Inf Bgde
- 4 OC A Coy
- 5   B
- 6   C
- 7   D
- 8 Adjt 3rd Batt 108th U S A Inf Rgt
- 9 Spare

SECRET   Copy No 2

Addendum to Operation Orders No 13 dated July 27th 1918

10 Officers per Coy & 1 NCO per platoon will remain
in the line 24 hours after relief

                                        (Sgd) C. H. BROMHEAD
28.7.18   2/Lt A/Adjt HORV

SECRET   Copy No. 1.

1. 11th Battn The Queen's Operation Order no 14.
Ry map Sheet 27 & 28   July 31st 1918

INTENTION 1. The Battalion will be relieved by
the 10th Battn R W Kents tomorrow
31st inst, commencing about 11-30 pm.
After being relieved, the Battn will
occupy L 28 d. area (Sheet 28)

DETAIL (a) 2. Companies will be relieved as follows:—
A will be relieved by B Coy 10th R W Kents
C "   "   "   "   A "   "   "
B) Positions now held by B & D Coys will
D) be vacated & will march off at a
time to be notified later.
I (American) will be relieved by D Coy R.W.K.
M ("   ) will move out & be at B H Q
10th R.W.K. at 10-30 pm.

(b) The guides of the 10th R W K will guide
their own platoons to their positions.

(c) The Officers & N.C.O's now with the American
Coys will remain with them for the tour
in the front line & will render every possible
assistance by advising & helping their
respective Unit Commanders.

(d) One American N.C.O. of the platoon in
KIMBERLEY TRENCH will be detailed to
remain for 24 hrs after relief.

(2)

(e) All defence schemes, programmes of work, Trench maps & stores will be handed over, and receipts in duplicate will be forwarded to the Adjutant by 2 pm 1st prox.

(f) Coy Commanders will be responsible that their areas are left scrupulously clean.

(g) All HQrs mess Kit, signalling equipment, Officers Trench Bundles etc, will be stacked on the road at Sheet 27 M.12.d.3.5 by 10.45 pm sharp, & will be loaded on two limbers as quickly as possible.

(h) The L.G. limbers for L Guns & mess Kit of A & C Coys will be at the Brigade dump at Sheet 27 M.6.c.2.3 at 1.0 am. Those of B & D Coys at their Coys HQ at 11.0 pm.

(i) After being relieved, Coys will march to WIPPENHOEK by platoons at 100x interval via ZEVECOTEN & RENINGHELST.

(j) The NCO's of platoons who went as advanced party will meet their Platoons at Cross roads at L.35.d.15.40 & guide them to their areas.

(k) One Class 1 Signaller of A & C Coys and 5 Signallers of BHQ will be detailed to remain as Visual signallers during the next tour. Those who are the most push will be detailed. These will report to the Adjutant 10th R.W.K. at 6 pm tomorrow.

(3)

(l) All empty Petrol tins will be carried out
(m) Completion of relief will be reported to
   B.H.Q at WIPPENHOEK by code word "SOLVED"
(n) Present B.H.Q will close on completion of
   relief & will reopen at WIPPENHOEK at
   the same time.
   Acknowledge.

                                    (Sgd) J.P. Newman
                                          Capt & Adjt
31/7/18   11th Batt. The Queens

Issued by signals at

Copy No 1 C O   Copy No 10 Adjt 3rd Batt W.Rif
  "   2   Adjt   "   11   QM & T.O
  "   3   A Coy   "   12   S O
  "   4   B   "   13   LGO & I.O
  "   5   C   "   14   M O
  "   6   D   "   15   10th R.W.R.
  "   7   123 Bgde   "   16   RSM
  "   8   I Coy USA   "   17   file
  "   9   M   USA   "   18   War Diary

APPENDIX I

1ST PHASE.

ZERO+0 TO ZERO+1.

2ND PHASE.

ZERO+1 TO ZERO+3.

3. PHASE.

ZERO+3 TO ZERO+5.

4 PHASE.

ZERO+5 TO ZERO+8.

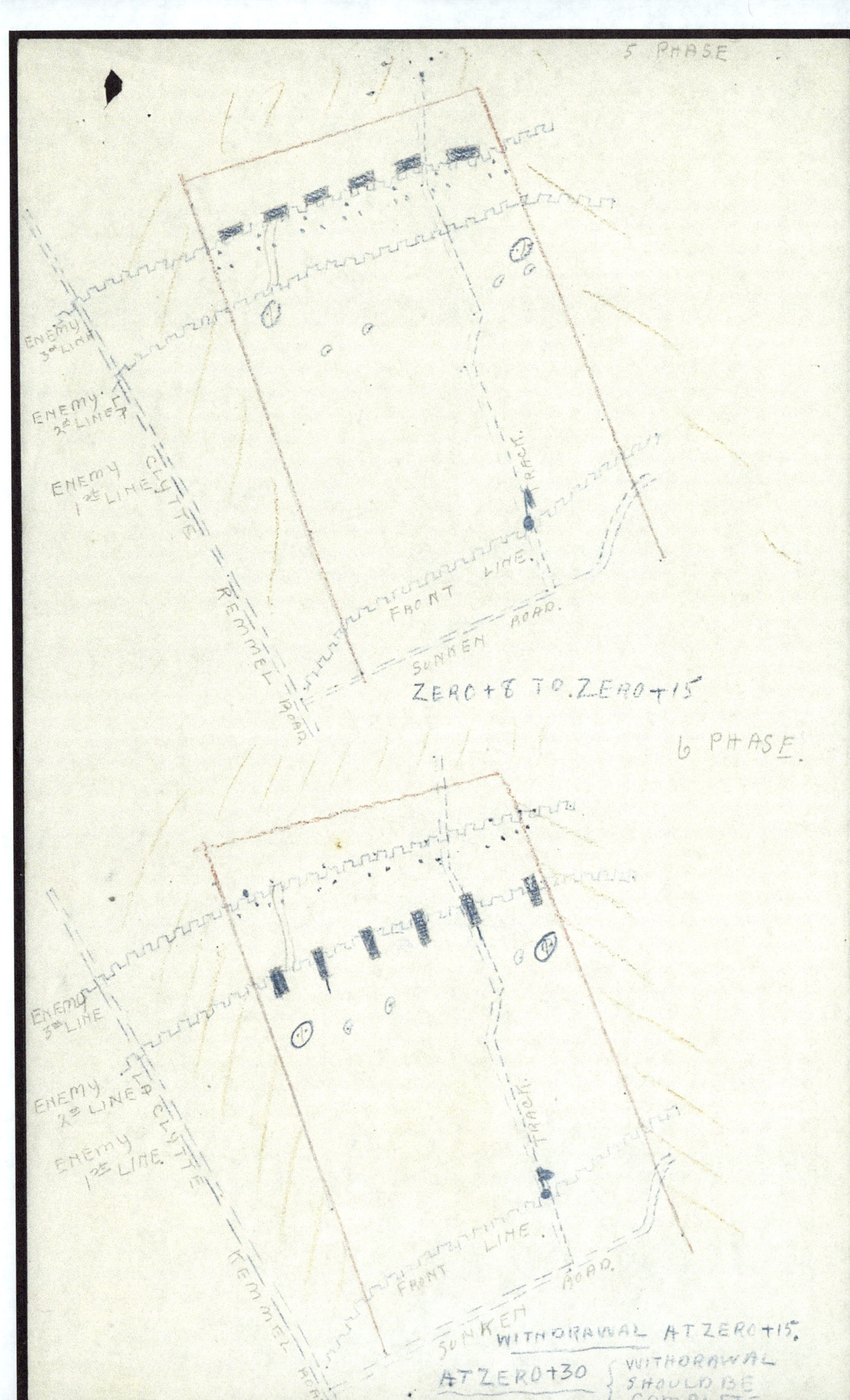

APPENDIX II.

DRESS and EQUIPMENT.

1. **DRESS.** — Clothing as issued.
   Steel Helmets.
   Box Respirators.

2. **ARMS.** — Rifles and Bayonets.

3. **AMMUNITION.** — 50 Rounds S.A.A. in bandolier tied round the waist per man.
   2 bombs per man. "moppers up" only. (Amendment)

4. **STRETCHER BEARERS.** — (a) Two Stretcher Bearers per Platoon to carry First Aid Requisites.

   (b) Each man to carry field dressing (shell).

5. **Lewis Guns.** — 8 Lewis Guns per Team.
   3 men to each gun.
   8 magazines to each gun.
   Spare parts bag to each gun.

All identifications to be removed previous to proceeding to the Assembly position.

Army Form C. 2118.

11 Q W Surrey Rgt
VOL 28

WAR DIARY
or
INTELLIGENCE SUMMARY
(Erase heading not required.)

Instructions regarding War Diaries and Intelligence Summaries are contained in F.S. Regs., Part II. and the Staff Manual respectively. Title pages will be prepared in manuscript.

Place	Date	Hour	Summary of Events and Information	Remarks and references to Appendices
LA CLYTTE	1st	2 am	Relieved in front line by 10th Bn. R.W. Kent Regt. Battalion proceeded to huttets in KLIPPE Area.	
		2 pm	Battalion bathed at Divl. Baths.	
		4.45 pm	Paraded and marched to ZEVECOTEN in Divl. Reserve. King Surprised at the disposal of G.O.C. 122nd Inf. Bde. Relieved 12th EAST SURREY Regt. Relief Complete 11.15 pm.	
ZEVECOTEN	2nd	—	Battalion found working parties on WESTOUTRE LINE and under R.E. from 122nd Inf. Bde.	
ZEVECOTEN	3rd	—	Working Parties as 2nd. 1 Officer (2Lt. C.H. Bromhead) and 12 N.C.Os & Men proceeded to TRANSPORT LINES to attend General parade at TERDEGHEM to 4th Army.	
ZEVECOTEN	4th	—	Working parties found for Front line under R.E. Slight shelling of Rendezvous Area during the afternoon. Casualties - nil.	
ZEVECOTEN	5th	—	Working parties as to 4th. The following Officer joined the Battalion. Major V. Holden D.S.O. M.C. R.W. Kent Regt. and assumed duties as 2nd in Chief of Battalion. Captain J.A.L. Horrocks returned from Davl. Reception Camp & assumed Command of "B" Coy.	

Army Form C. 2118.

WAR DIARY
or
INTELLIGENCE SUMMARY.
(Erase heading not required.)

Instructions regarding War Diaries and Intelligence Summaries are contained in F.S. Regs., Part II. and the Staff Manual respectively. Title pages will be prepared in manuscript.

August 1918

Place	Date	Hour	Summary of Events and Information	Remarks and references to Appendices
ZEVECOTEN	6th		Working Parties found for Bath Lines under R.E. The following Officers joined the Battalion and were posted to Coys. as follows:- Lieut W. MAY. "A" Coy; Lieut. G.L. GUNN "B" Coy; Lieut. H.M. TODD "C" Coy. 3 O.R. wounded. Operation Orders received from Bde reported Relief	See Operation Orders attached
ZEVECOTEN	7th		Relieved by 16th Bn. Hants Regt. and Battalion proceeded to LAPPE Area. Relief and move completed at 2.30 a.m.	
LAPPE	8th		Battalion bathed and cleaned up generally.	
LAPPE	9th		Battalion carried on training from 9 a.m. to 12.30 p.m. and was inspected an training by Divl. Comdr. (Major Gen. Sir SYDNEY T.B. LAWFORD K.C.B.) Operation Order for relief and attachment of 2nd Bn. 107th Regt. U.S.A. received.	
LAPPE	10th		H. 2nd Bn 107th Regt U.S.A. arrived at 2 p.m. and the Battalion was organised into 2 Battns, 50 p.c. British, 50 p.c. American in each, known as "A" & "B" Composite Battalions. "A" Battn. Composed of "A" & "B" Coys attached "C" & "D" Coys. Queens - "E" & "F" Coys Americans. "B" Battalion "C" & "D" Coys Queens- "G" & "H" Coys Americans. P.T.O.	C.O.R.

Army Form C. 2118.

WAR DIARY
or
INTELLIGENCE SUMMARY.
(Erase heading not required.)

August 1918.

Place	Date	Hour	Summary of Events and Information	Remarks and references to Appendices
LAPPE	10th		Coys were numbers in Battalions as follows :- "A" Batt: A1, A2, A3, A4. "B" Batt: B1, B2, B3, B4. "A" Battalion paraded and marched off at 8.15 p.m. and moved into Front Line Guilfy Scala and relieved 101st Inf. Regt. U.S.A. Rely Complete at 2.25 a.m. 11th inst. "B" Battalion paraded and marched off at 8.45 p.m. and moved into Support position in Cula Scala relieving the 28th Bn. Middlesex Regt. Relief Complete at 1.15 a.m. 11th inst. Casualties 1 O.R. - Killed, 1 O.R. wounded.	
LA PIATTE	11th		After a barrage the enemy attacked the left Brigade Sects. at 4.30 a.m. Part of the enemy barrage fell on our left from his Coy. The advance of enemy repulsed by Lt. Vee. Day remains quiet. Casualties 4 O.R. wounded.	
LA PIATTE	12th		A counter preparation was carried out by our Artillery at 3.15 a.m. Day quiet at Pt. R "A" Batt. reorganized into 2 Coys + Btalts (S.H.) Disposition "A" Coy + 2 Coys American Companies as follows: "A" Queeno, Right Front, "C" American - Left Front, "H" Coy American - FERMOY FARM. "B" Coy Queeno. SUPPORT. Casualties - American - 1 Killed, 4 wounded. British -	

Army Form C. 2118.

WAR DIARY
or
INTELLIGENCE SUMMARY. AUGUST 1918.

(Erase heading not required.)

Instructions regarding War Diaries and Intelligence Summaries are contained in F.S. Regs, Part II. and the Staff Manual respectively. Title pages will be prepared in manuscript.

Place	Date	Hour	Summary of Events and Information	Remarks and references to Appendices
LA CLYTTE	13th		A counter preparation by the enemy artillery was made at 2am. Also a preparation was put down by our artillery at 3.10 am. — May fired Rifles of "A" Bath, by "B" Bath. Commenced at 10.30 pm. 1 OR Killed, 4 OR Wounded.	
LA CLYTTE	14th		Relief completed by 12.30 am. Dispositions as follows: B1. Left Front. B2. Right Front. B3. FERMOY FARM. B4. Support. HQRS P Review, RSM HQ. assumed Command of "B" Bath. Capt Fantadowne assumed command of "A" Bath. On completion of relief Bath HQ. was not relieved. Dispositions of "A" Battalion on relief were :- A Coy Queens and B Coy Americans. SCHERPENBURG LINE. "B" Coy Queens & H Coy Americans REDOUBT LINE. Day quiet. 1 OR Killed, 1 OR Wounded. 1 Rule 2 wounded. Canadian.	
LA CLYTTE	16th		Slight shelling of front line with T.Ms during the day. Re-organization into 2 complete Lewis Guns and 2 Lewis Guns Coys "B" Battalion commenced at dusk. Dispositions as follows: "E" Coy Queens Left Front. "C" Coy Queens Right Front. "F" Coy Americans FERMOY FARM. "D" Coy Queens Support. Relief completed at 1.10 am. 1 OR Wounded. Canadian. 2 OR's & OR's 8 OR's Wounded.	

Army Form C. 2118.

WAR DIARY August 1918.
or
INTELLIGENCE SUMMARY.
(Erase heading not required.)

Instructions regarding War Diaries and Intelligence Summaries are contained in F.S. Regs., Part II. and the Staff Manual respectively. Title pages will be prepared in manuscript.

Place	Date	Hour	Summary of Events and Information	Remarks and references to Appendices
LA CLYTTE	16th	—	Bn. HQrs. was shelled at 10.15 a.m. for half an hour, otherwise day was quiet. At dusk the 2nd Bn. 107th Infy. U.S.A. took over the Front line "C" & "D" Coys being relieved by G & H Coys American. Relief was complete at 12.15 a.m. Bn HQ moved from J/M.12.d.90.36 to J/N.4.c. 15-25. Hqrs. HEDGE STREET. Casualties 14 OR wounded. (British Army)	
LA CLYTTE	17th		Working parties under R.E. and on defences were carried out during the day and night. Slight shelling around Support line during the day, also gas shells were dropped round Bn HQ at 11.30 p.m. Casualties Nil.	
LA CLYTTE	18th		Working Parties continuing work on defences and under R.E. Day quiet except for occasional shelling on our O.P. Casualties 4 Killed & Wounded * OR Killed 4 Wounded	
LA CLYTTE	19th		Working Parties continued work on defences and under R.E. Day quiet. Occasional shelling. Casualties Nil.	

WAR DIARY or INTELLIGENCE SUMMARY

Army Form C. 2118.

(Erase heading not required.)

Instructions regarding War Diaries and Intelligence Summaries are contained in F.S. Regs., Part II. and the Staff Manual respectively. Title Pages will be prepared in manuscript.

Place	Date	Hour	Summary of Events and Information	Remarks and references to Appendices
LA CLYTTE	20th	—	Working parties continued on defences and were R.E's. Slight shelling during the day, including gas on the H.Q's and Coy areas. Lt Colonel M.L. Owen M.C. returned from leave and assumed the command of the Battalion.	
LA CLYTTE	21st		Working parties continued on defences as usual. R.S. Day Quiet. Notification received that the following decorations had been awarded for the raid on 18/19th July 1916. MILITARY CROSS:- CAPT. F.L. FURNESS. LIEUT. F.S. TROTTER D.C.M. LIEUT. D. MOON. LIEUT. D. JACKSON. DISTINGUISHED CONDUCT MEDAL 11290 CORPL J. FINLAYSON. Casualties R.R. [?]	
LA CLYTTE	22nd		Working parties as usual. Day quiet. Slight shelling of Reserve Line about 10 p.m. 2 O.R. Killed.	
LA CLYTTE	23rd		Relief of Support Batt'n to Outer Lines commenced, "C" & "B" Coy relieving "D" Coy. 23rd Aus Regt. made in "B" Coy relieving "A" Coy Right Front. Coy remain in such "A" Coy keep Right occupied position in Left Support. 1 O.R. wounded.	

Army Form C. 2118.

WAR DIARY
or
INTELLIGENCE SUMMARY

(Erase heading not required.)

Instructions regarding War Diaries and Intelligence Summaries are contained in F. S. Regs., Part II. and the Staff Manual respectively. Title Pages will be prepared in manuscript.

Place	Date	Hour	Summary of Events and Information	Remarks and references to Appendices
LA CLYTTE	24		Shells dropped over front lines at 3.40 am and gradually spread to our front. Remainder of day quiet, after it was reported that enemy's Southern Column took place on left at that section. Reinf. Bn. Coy relief took place at 11 pm between "C" & "D" Coys. 4 O.R. wounded	
LA CLYTTE	25	11 am	Above relief complete at 1.30 am. Hostile shelling on Bn. H.Q. & working parties as usual. Otherwise quiet. 1 O.R. wounded	
LA CLYTTE	26		Working parties been employed on defences — wire &c. At dusk the occupation of the line was continued, our 129th/Div. took over the left sector of the West Section, the Bn. Southern Boundary remaining through 28/N.134.40.26. N.Y.C.+4.7.N.+3.61. B Coy. handed over the position held by 26th Bn. to 26th Royal Fusiliers. A. Coy. were relieved in Support. C. Coy. relieved the 28th Middlesex in KIMBERLEY TRENCH on the platoon in SNOB TRENCH by 26th R. Fus. but now took over position on right. One platoon one O.R. wounded. 2 O.R. wounded	AA24
LA CLYTTE	27		Enemy exploded at 2.15 pm shells heavily Southern Slope of Support Trench bombing centres as usual. Slightly heavier shelling of Support Trench during the afternoon. Otherwise quiet.	

Army Form C. 2118.

WAR DIARY
or
INTELLIGENCE SUMMARY
(Erase heading not required.)

Instructions regarding War Diaries and Intelligence Summaries are contained in F. S. Regs., Part II. and the Staff Manual respectively. Title Pages will be prepared in manuscript.

Place	Date	Hour	Summary of Events and Information	Remarks and references to Appendices
LA CLYTTE	28.	—	Working parties as usual. Slight shelling in Battn Area. Received orders for the relief on 29th inst. Slept per return form in B.H.Q.	
LA CLYTTE	29.		Day quiet. At night the Battalion was relieved by 2/4th Bn. The Queens Regt. "A" Coy was relieved by "D" Coy Qns. "B" Coy by "C" Coy Qns. "C" Coy Qns. "D" Coy by "A" Coy Qns. "B" Coy Qns. 1 OR Killed 4OR wounded.	
LOVE	30.		Relief completed at 1.05 am, and Battalion marched to LOVE where it halted for a few hours. At 6 a.m. at entrained on light Rly at LOVE and travelled to WINNEZEELE where a halt was made for 3 hours. Afterwards entraining on M.G. Railway and proceeding to ST MOMELIN within the environs and marched to billets at TATINGHEM. Bivouacs here at 6 pm.	
TATINGHEM	31/8		The day was spent in cleaning and fitting up our equipment. Several programmes courses and detail given out regarding the Coys actives at rest.	

W. N. Wall
Lt. Colonel
Comdg 11th Bn The Queens Ry

ADDENDA TO
OPERATION ORDER No N.

All defence schemes, trench maps, programmes of work, trench stores etc, will be taken over, receipts obtained & duplicates forwarded to Batt HQrs by 2 pm on the 2nd inst.

(Sgd) T P NEWMAN
Capt & Adjt
11th Queens

Issued to all recipients.

SECRET   Copy No 1
          11th Batt. The Queens' Operation Order No 15
Ref map Sheets 27 & 28   Aug 1st 1918

INTENTION.   1 The Battn. will relieve the 12th East
                Surreys in the left sector reserve
                positions in the WESTOUTRE – GOED
                MOET MILL LINE, on the night of
                the 1st/2nd August

DETAIL   2 Coys & platoons will relieve their
                opposite numbers.

ORDER OF
  MARCH   3 Batt HQrs, C, B, D & A.

STARTING PT 4 27/L 35 a 9.8

TIME   5 Head of column to pass starting point
                at 7-45 pm.

ROUTE   6 27/L 35 d 2.3 & main road to 28/G 32 d 8.3

GUIDES   7 1 Guide per platoon, 1 guide per
                Coy HQrs, & 1 guide per Batt HQrs
                will be at 28/G 32 d 8.3 at 9.15 pm
                & will guide their respective units
                to their positions.

RATIONS   8 As usual

TRANSPORT   9 Two limbers will report at Batt
                HQrs at 7-15 pm for trench bundles
                & mess gear.
                Companies will arrange to have
                their trench bundles & mess boxes

(2)

dumped at Batt HQrs at 7-30pm & to fetch them from reserve Batt HQrs 28/9 35 a 8 2 after arrival.

L.G. Limbers will report to their respective Coys at 7.15 pm & move off in rear of their respective leading platoons

10. Batt HQrs will close here at 7-45 pm & open at the same hour at 28/9 35 a 8 2

11. Completion of relief will be reported to Batt HQrs 28/9 35 a 8 2 by runners

12. Acknowledge

(Sgd) T.P. NEWMAN
Capt & adjt.
11th Queens.

Issued by runners at

Copy no 1 C.O   no 9 I O & S O
        2 Adj   10 M O & L G O
        3 123 Inf Bgde   11 R S M
        4 OC A Coy   12 WAR DIARY
        5   B   13 FILE
        6   C   14 SPARE
        7   D
        8 Lt Qmr & T O

S E C R E T. *Adjutant.* Copy No. 3

ADDENDUM TO OPERATION ORDER No. 16.

11th Bn. "The Queen's" (RWS) Regiment.

7th August 1918.

1. Empty petrol tins will be stacked with cooking utensils at Bn.H.Q.

2. Reference Para. 2. Os.C.Coys. will report in person.

ACKNOWLEDGE.

(Sd) T.P. NEWMAN.
Capt. & Adjt.
11th Bn. "The Queen's" (RWS) Regt.

Issued at 5.10 p.m.
Issued to all recipients of O.O.16 dated 7-8-18.

SECRET. 2nd i/c.   Copy No. 2

<u>ADDENDUM TO OPERATION ORDER No.16.</u>

<u>11th Bn. "The Queen's" (RWS) Regiment.</u>

<u>7th August 1918.</u>

1. Empty petrol tins will be stacked with cooking utensils at Bn.H.Q.

2. Reference Para 2. Os.C.Coys. will report in person.

<u>ACKNOWLEDGE.</u>

                                     (Sd) T.P. NEWMAN.
                                          Capt. & Adjt.
                        11th Bn. "The Queen's" (RWS) Regt.

Issued at 5.10 p.m.
Issued to all recipients of O.O.16 dated 7-8-18.

SECRET.   Copy No....... 1

OPERATION ORDER No.16.
11th Bn. "The Queen's" (RWS) Regt.

Ref. Map Sheet 27 & 28.   7th August 1918.

INTENTION.	1.	The Battalion will be relieved tonight 7th inst. by the 15th Hampshire Regt. Relief will commence between 9 p.m. and 10 p.m. On being relieved Coys. will march to billets in 27/L.30 Area. Platoons will march at intervals of 50 yards.
RELIEF.	2.	Os.C.Coys. will report their relief complete to Bn.H.Q.
GUIDES.	3.	Guides at the rate of 1 per Platoon and Coy.H.Q. will report to R.S.M. at Bn.H.Q. at 9 p.m.
TRANSPORT.	4.	Three Limbers will be at Bn.H.Q. at 10 p.m. for Trench Bundles, H.Q.Mess Kit, Signalling Equipment etc., and cooking utensils of the Battalion: all cooking utensils will be stacked outside Bn.H.Q. by 9.45 p.m. L.G.Limbers will pick up Lewis Guns, Coy.Trench Bundles, and Mess Kit at Bn.H.Q.
AREA.	5.	Os.C.Coys. will ensure that their Areas are left in a perfectly clean and sanitary condition.
TRENCH STORES.	6.	Trench Stores, Maps, etc. will be handed over and receipts in duplicate forwarded to the Adjutant by 2 p.m. tomorrow 8th inst.
PETROL TINS.	7.	Empty petrol tins will be carried out.
B.H.Q.	8.	Present Bn.H.Q. will close on completion of relief and will re-open at L.30 Area at the same time.

ACKNOWLEDGE.

(Sd) T.P. NEWMAN.
Capt. & Adjutant.
11th Bn. "The Queen's" (RWS) Regt.

Issued at 1.45 p.m.

```
Copy No.  1. - C.O.
  "    "  2. - 2nd i/c.
  "    "  3. - Adjutant.
  "    "  4. - "A" Coy.
  "    "  5. - "B"  "
  "    "  6. - "C"  "
  "    "  7. - "D"  "
  "    "  8. - 123rd Inf.Bde.
  "    "  9. - 122nd Inf.Bde.
  "    " 10. - Q.M. and T.O.
  "    " 11. - Signalling Officer.
  "    " 12. - Lewis Gun Officer.
  "    " 13. - Medical Officer.
  "    " 14. - R.S.M.
  "    " 15. - File.
  "    " 16. - War Diary.
```

SECRET.   Copy No. 4

OPERATION ORDER No. 17.
11th Bn. "Queen's" R. W. S. Regt.

Ref. Map Sheet 27.

1. **INTENTION.**
   Companies will move into billets at present occupied by the 10th R. W. Kent Regt. tonight, and will be ready to move off at 8.30pm. Coys. will move independently. Battalion Hd. Qrs. will remain in its present position.

2. **DETAIL.**
   Coys. will take over as follows:-
   A. Coys. "Queen's" from C. Coy. R.W.Kent. Regt.
   B. "   "   -- " B. "   "   "   "
   C. "   "   " A. "   "   "   "
   D. "   "   " D. "   "   "   "

3. **RELIEF.**
   Completion of relief will be notified to Bn. H.Qrs. by runner.

4. **SANITATION.**
   O.s. C. Coys. will ensure that their billets are left in a clean and sanitary condition and will render a Certificate to the Adjutant to that effect, also a certificate will be rendered to the effect that the billets taken over by them from the R.W. Kent Regt. are in a clean and sanitary condition.

5. **TRANSPORT.**
   All valises, Mess kit, etc. will be moved under Coy. arrangements. Limbers that are coming with rations will be utilized.

6. **ACKNOWLEDGE.**

   Copy issued to :-

   No. 1. C.O.   No.10. L.G.O
       2. Adjt.   11. M.O.
       3. O.C. A. Coy.   12. R.S.M.
       4. O.C. B. Coy.   13. File.
       5. O.C. C. Coy.   14. War Diary.
       6. O.C. D. Coy.
       7. 123rd Inf. Brigade.
       8. Q.M. and T.O.
       9. S.B.

8-8-18.   (Sgd) T.P.NEWMAN.
                                            Capt. & Adjt.
                                          11th Bn. "The Queen's" Regt.

SECRET.   Copy No. 21

OPERATION ORDER No. 17.   10th August 1918
11th Bn. "The Queen's" Regt.

Reference Map Sheets 27 and 28.

1. **INTENTION.**
   Two Composite Battalions, each composed of two Companies of 11th Bn. "The Queen's" Regt and two Companies of Americans will take over the Centre Sector, Front and Support Line, tonight, the 10th inst

2. **ORGANISATION.**
   The two Battalions will be known as "A" and "B" Battalions respectively and will be composed as follows:-

   Headquarters. "A" Battalion.
   Major V. HOLDEN. D.S.O. M.C.   Commanding Officer.
   Capt. & Adjt. T.P. NEWMAN.   Adjutant.
   Lieut. J. COWAN.   L.G. and Works Officer.
   2/Lieut. G. CONWAY.   Signalling & Gas Officer.
   R.S.M. Mahoney.
   9 Signallers.   4 Pioneers.
   5 Observers.   7 Runners.

   A. 1. Coy.
   Lieut. A. W. HOOLEY. M.C.   Company Commander.
   2/Lieut. W.E. HUNTER.
   1 Officer of R.W. Kent Regt.
   1 Senior and 4 Junior N.C.Os of R.W. Kent Regt.
   Nos. 1 & 2 Platoons. "A" Coy.
   2 Platoons.   U.S. Army.

   A. 2. Coy.
   1 Officer R.W. Kent Regt.   Company Commander.
   2/Lieut. J.W. DENTON.
   1 Senior & 4 Junior N.C.Os of R.W. Kent Regt.
   Nos. 3 & 4 Platoons "A" Coy.
   2 Platoons   U.S. Army.

   A. 3. Coy.
   2/Lieut. F. A. COLLINS.   Company Commander.
   "   E. J.W. NEAVE.
   "   S.J. de la MOTHE.
   Nos. 5 & 6 Platoons. B. Coy.
   2 Platoons U.S. Army.
   1 Senior and 4 Junior N.C.Os R.W. Kent Regt.

   A. 4. Company.
   2/Lieut. N.A. SKELTON.   Company Commander.
   "   E. BURCHETT.
   1 Officer of R. W. Kent Regt.
   1 Senior and 4 Junior N.C.Os of R.W. Kent Regt.
   Nos. 7 & 8 Platoons. B. Coy.
   2 Platoons U. S. Army.

   Headquarters "B" Battalion.
   Capt. J.A.L. HOPKINSON.   Commanding Officer.
   2/Lieut. C.H. BROMHEAD.   A/Adjutant.
   Sergt. Coward.   A/R.S.M.
   Signalling Sergeant and 8 Signallers.
   2 Pioneers, 4 Observers and 8 Runners.

   B. 1. Coy.
   Lieut. L.C.E. BAKER. M.C.   Company Commander.
   2/Lieut. W. HAY.
   1 Officer of Middlesex Regt.
   1 Senior and 4 Junior N.C.Os of Middx. Regt.
   Nos. 9 & 10 Platoons. "C" Coy.
   2 Platoons U.S. Army.

A. 2. Coy.
1 Officer of the Middx. Regt.   Company Commander.
1   "   "   "   "   "
Lieut. F. M. TODD.
1 Senior and 4 Junior N.C.Os of Middx. Regt.
Nos. 11 & 12 Platoons.   "C" Coy.
2 Platoons. U.S. Army.

B. 3. Coy.
Lieut. R. F. EDWARDS.   Company Commander.
2/Lieut. G.L. GUNN.
1 Senior and 4 Junior N.C.Os of Middx. Regt.
Nos. 13 & 14 Platoons.   D. Coy.
2 Platoons.   U.S. Army.

nB. 4. Coy.
Lieut. C.C. PRESCOTT.   Company Commander.
1 Officer of the Middx. Regt.
1 Senior and 4 Junior N.C.Os of Middx. Regt.
Nos. 15 & 16 Platoons.   "D" Coy.
2 Platoons. U.S. Army.

3. DETAIL.
The relief will be carried out as follows:-
"A" Battalion will take over the front line from 168th Infantry Regt, U.S.Army.
    A. 1. Coy.   Left Front.
    A. 2. "   Right Front.
    A. 3. "   Fermoy Farm.
    A. 4. "   Support.
Guides for above will be met at 28/I.33.35.2C. at 10.30pm

"B" Battalion will relieve the 23rd Middx. Regt. in support:-
    B. 1. Coy. will relieve A. Coy. Middx. Regt. in left front.
    B. 2. Coy. will relieve B. Coy. Middx. Regt. in right
                                                    support.
    B. 3. Coy. "   "   C. "   "   " in right front.
    B. 4. Coy. "   "   D. "   "   " in left support
Guides will meet "B" Battalion at 28/M.5.a.1.5. at 10.30pm.

4. MOVE.
"A" Battalion will parade ready to move past starting point, "DARLINGTON CAMP" 27/L.30.c.8.2, at 8.15 pm.
Order of march - A.1. A.2. A.3. A.4.- Platoons
at intervals of 50 yards.
"B" Battalion will be ready to move past starting point at "DARLINGTON CAMP" 27/L.29.c.8.2. at 9.15 pm.
Order of March - B.1. - B.2. B.3. - B.4. Platoons at 50 yds interval
Dress Fighting Order.
Packs and Greatcoats to be clearly labelled and stacked outside of Coys. H.Q. and collected under arrangements of Q.M.

5. RATIONS.
Rations for 11th inst. will be carried in on the man. Ration dumps whilst in the line will be:-
    Front Line Battalion.   28/M.17.d.1.5.
    Support Battalion.   28/M.12.a.7.5.
Ration parties will be detailed daily by Coys. as follows:-
    A. 1. Coy.   10 men.
    A. 2. "   10 "
    A. 3. "   20 men
    A. 4. "   20 men.
to carry for Front Line Coys.. "A" 4. Coy. will arrange to carry their own rations.
Ration arrangements for "B" Battalion will be made by O.C. "B" Batt.

6. TRENCH STORES ETC.
All Defence Schemes (except the Brigade Defence Scheme) Progress Reports on Work, and sketches, Programmes of work, permanent working party details, Trench Maps and Stores, information obtained by patrols etc. will be taken over on relief. Receipts will be obtained in duplicate and sent to the Adjt. as soon as possible after the relief is complete.

3.

WORK.
Works reports, accompanied with map will be taken over and forwarded to the Adjutant as soon as relief is complete.

TRANSPORT.
Lewis Guns will be taken up on Limbers and will be unloaded at the following points:-
"A" Battalion. 28/M.12.d.1.5.
"B"   "   28/M.12.a.7.5.
Two Limbers for H.Q. Mess kit, Signalling Equipment etc. will be unloaded at 28/M.12.d.1.5. These stores will be loaded at Battn. H.Q. at 7 pm.
Officers Valises will be stacked at Battn. & Coy. H.Q. at 7.30pm.

9. **RELIEF.**
Os. C. Coys. will report relief complete by runner.
Code word "JIMMY".

10. **BILLETS.**
Os. C. Coys. will ensure that all billets and bivouacs are left in a clean and sanitary condition and will render a certificate to the Adjutant. to that effect.

                                        (sgd) T. P. NEWMAN.
                                            Capt. & Adjt.
                                    11th Bn. "The Queen's" Regt.

Copy issued to :-
  No. 1. C.O.
      2. Adjt.
      3. A. 1 Coy.
      4. A. 2   "
      5. A. 3   "
      6. A. 4   "
      7. O.C. "B" Battn.
      8. A/Adjt. "B" Battn.
      9. B. 1 Coy.
    10. B. 2 Coy.
    11. B. 3 Coy.
    12. B. 4 Coy.
    13. QM. & TO.
    14. S.O.

15. M.O.
16. L.G.O.
17. R.S.M.
18. O.C. American Bn.
19. 133rd Infantry Bde.
20. A/R.S.M. "B" Bn.
21. File.
22. War Diary.

SECRET.   Copy No.

OPERATION ORDER. No.19"
11th Bn. "Queen's" Regt.
                                                            12-8-18 .

Ref.
Map Sheet 28.

1. **INTENTION.**
   "A" Composite Battalion will be relieved in the front line by
   "B" Composite Battalion tomorrow night, 13th inst.
   Relief to commence about 10.30pm.

2. **DETAIL.**
   "B" Battalion will take over positions as follows:-
       B.1. Coy. will relieve G. Coy. Americans in Left Front.
       B.2. "   "   "   A. "   "Queen's" in Right Front.
       B.3. "   "   "   H. "   Americans in FERMOY FARM.
       B.4. "   "   "   B. "   "Queen's" in Support.
   The Signallers of B.1. and B.2. Coys. will relieve the
   signallers at present employed with G. Coy. Americans and
   A. Coy. "Queen's" The Signallers employed at FERMOY FARM and
   Support will not be relieved.

3. **GUIDES.**
   Guides from A. Coy. "Queen's", G and H. Coys. Americans,
   on the scale of 1 per platoon and Coy. H.Q. will be sent down to
   Bn. H.Q. tonight and will report at Bn. H.Q.
   Os. C. Coys. will make arrangements to have a guide from each
   post at their platoons Headquarters to meet platoons.

4. **MOVES.**
   On completion of relief "A" Battalion will move into support
   positions as follows:-
       A. Coy. "Queen's"   Right Front.
       B. "   "   Right Support.
       G. "   Americans. Left Front.
       H. "   "   Left Support.

5. **TRENCH STORES. ETC.**
   All trench stores etc. will be handed over and receipts
   forwarded to Bn. H.Q. immediately after relief.
   All maps, sketches of dispositions, and sketch work in hand
   and proposed will be handed over and receipts taken.

6. **DESIGNATION.**
   The completion of relief will be reported to the respective
   Battalion H.Q. The present Front line Battalion will be known as
   "B" Battalion and the present Support Battalion as "A" Battalion.
   CODE WORD "SAM"

7. **HEADQUARTERS.**
   The Battalions' H. Qrs. will remain as at present.

8. **WORK.**
   After the relief is completed, the front line battalion
   will vigourously continue work handed over.

9. **RATIONS.**
   Os. C. Coys. will hand over present system of carrying rations.

10. **ATTACHMENT.**
    Each Coy. will leave one Officer per Coy. and one Senior N.C.O
    per platoon in the line for 24 hours after the relief.

                                            Capt. & Adjt.
                                        11th Bn. "The Queen's" Regt

SECRET.

OPERATION ORDER. No. 30.
11th Bn. "The Queen's" Regt.   13th August 1918.

Ref.
Ma. Ma. Sheet. 28.

1. **INTENTION.**
   In accordance with the organisation for the 2nd Leg and 3rd Days i.e. 15th and 16th instant., the following will be carried out :-
   A. From "Stand To" on the morning of the 15th inst., 50% of the platoons will be commanded by an American Platoon Officer. This will necessitate every American Platoon Officer having a command. The name of the Officer and the platoon he commands will be forwarded to Bn. H.Q. before dawn on the 15th inst.
   B. On the night 15/16th inst.s the Battalion will reorganise into two complete American Companies and two British Companies.

2. **DETAIL.**
   The positions to be occupied will be as follows :-
   Coy. E. American   - Left Front.
   Coy.D.Queen's   - Right
   "C" Coy. "Queen's"   - Right Front.
   Coy. F. American.   - PERRY FARM.
   "D" Coy. "Queen's"   - Support.
   Owing to the numerical difference in strength of American and British Coys, O. C. "E" Coy. will take over the left platoon sector of the right front Coy.

3. **GUIDES.**
   Guides will be sent to reconnoitre as under on the night 15/16th inst., and after reconnoisance they will rejoin their present Coy. O. C. B.1. Coy will send to B. 2. Coy. a British guide for each post. O. C. B.2. Coy. will send to B.1. Coy. an American guide and 1 British guide for each post, with exception of the left platoon. O. C. B.3. Coy. will send to B.4 Coy 1 a British guide per platoon. O. C. B.4. Coy. will send to B.3. Coy. 1 American and 1 British guide per platoon.

4. **MOVE.**
   The following procedure will be adopted for carrying out the move :-
   10.30pm. All Americans are withdrawn from B.3. Coy. and take up positions on left front, when completed the British contingent will move from B.1. Coy. into Right Front.
   10.15pm. All Americans will move from B.4. Coy. to positions in PERRY FARM and when completed, all British Troops in B.3. Coy will move into position in Support.

5. **ATTACHMENTS.**
   Os. C. Coys C and D. Coys., will each detail One Officer per Coy. and one N.C.O. per platoon to be attached to E and F. Coys. Americans. These Officers and N.C.Os. will do all in their power to assist the American Coy. and Platoon Commanders by giving them advice on all matters, but will not take command.

6. **TRENCH STORES etc.**
   Os. C. B.1 and B.3. Coys will ensure that all stores, maps, work in hand and proposed, are properly handed over and also information regarding intelligence. The present system of carrying rations will also be handed over. Receipts will be taken.

7. **PATROLS.**
   Defensive Patrols will be put out by the Front Companies whilst the move is taking place, and will be withdrawn after completion.

8. **REPORTS.**
   Completion of move will be sent to Bn. H.Q. by runner. Code Word "SIMPLE".

9. **WORK.**
   The work will be continued vigourously as soon as the move is completed.

                                                   Capt. & Adjt.

BATTALION ORDERS. No.
Copy No. 2
By.
Lieut. Col. W. L. OWEN. M.C. Cmdg. 11th Bn. "The Queen's" Regt. 27-8-18

Ref. Sheet. 27.

1. INTENTION.   The Brigade will move to the St. MARTIN AU LAERT sub-area on 29/30th August 1918. The 11th Bn. "The Queen's" Regt. will be accomodated at TATINGHEM. The journey will be made by light railway.

2. DETAIL.   The Battalion on being relelved will march to LOYE, where it will entrain as follows :-

Train.	Coys.	Time.	Change at	Detrain
No.1.	A & B.	6.12am	WINNEZEELE.	at
No.2.	C.D.& H.Q.	6.15am	"	MOMELIN.
No.3.	(Surplus Personnel)	6.20am	"	"
	Odd	"	)	

Nos. 1 and 2 trains consist of 12 trucks, No.3 of 13 trucks each accomodating 30 all ranks.
Lieut. Hooley.M.C. will act as entraining Officer for the Battalion and will reconnoitre the entraining point tomorrow afternoon.
After detraining at St. MOMELIN, the Battalion will proceed to TATINGHEM by march route.

3. ADVANCE PARTY.   An advanced party if 5 N.C.Os. to be detailed by O.C. Details Camp, under the command of 2/Lieut. CH. BROMHEAD will proceed to St. MARTIN AU LAERT by lorry leaving Embussing Point at K.34.c.9.3. at 6 am on the 29th inst. They will report to the Staff Captain or representative at the Area Cmmdts Office about 11am.

4. TRENCH BUNDLES, etc.   ONly light trench bundles can be taken on the trains. Os.C. Coys. and Specialists Officers will therefire arrange to send all surplus kits, mess kit etc. down to the transport lines tonight

5. TRANSPORT.   Extra limbers will come up tonight to take down all surplus kits, signalling equipment, gas clothing etc.
The trabsport less L.G. Limbers will move to new area by march route on 29th inst. under the orders of O.C. No.3 Train.A.S.C.
The L.G. Limbers will remain behind to bring Lewis Guns from the line tomorrow night 29th inst under the command of Lieut.C.C.Prescott. They will proceed by same route as 1st Line Transport.

6. RATIONS.   Rations for consumption on 29th inst. and 30th will be issued tonight

7. STRENGTH.   Os. C. Coys.etc. will render a return to the Adjutant by 5am. 30th inst. showing the actual number of Officers and Other Ranks proceeding by train.

8. DETAILS.   All details now at the Details Camp will report to the Adjutant at the entraining point at 5.30am

9. SANITATION.   Os. C. Coys. will ensure that the railway trucks etc. are left clean on detrainment.

10. WATER.   All water bottles. will if possible, be filled prior to entrainment.

11. MEALS.   The Quartermaster will arrange to have a hot meal reafy at the detraining point.

(Sgd)T.P.NEWMAN.
- Capt. & Adjt.
11th Bn. "The Queen's"regt.

S E C R E T.   Copy No. 2

OPERATION ORDER No. 86.
11th Bn. "The Queen's" Regt.

Ref: Map Sheet. 27 S.E.   28th August 1918.

1. INTENTION.   The 153rd Infantry Brigade will be relieved by the
                   101st Infantry Brigade on the night 29/30th inst.
                   The Battalion will be relieved by the 2/4th Bn.
                   "The Queen's" Regt. On being relieved the Coys.
                   and Bn.H.Q. personnel will march independently to
                   the LOKE Area for entrainment to St MARTIN AU
                   LAERT Area. Lt. Hooley M.C." will meet platoons
                   at this area and show them where their meal will
                   be served.

2. DETAILS.   Coys. will be relieved as follows :-
                   Front Line Coy.   by B. Coy. 2/4th Queen's.
                   Sch. Dick. Lake Line Coy. by A. Coy. 2/4th Queen's
                   Right Support Coy.   " D. "   "
                   Left   "   "   " C. "   "

3. PERSONNEL TO   1 officer and 1 N.C.O. per platoon will remain
   BE LEFT BEHIND. with the relieving Battalion for 24 hours after
                   relief. Instructions regarding rejoining Battalion
                   will be issued later.

4. TRENCH STORES. ALL Defence Schemes, programmes of work, under
                   construction and proposed, trench maps and stores,
                   information obtained by patrols, A.A. posts etc. will
                   be handed over on relief. Receipts will be obtained
                   in duplicate and forwarded to the Orderly Room
                   as soon as possible after relief.

5. TRANSPORT.   Lewis Gun limbers will be at the ration dump at
                   10pm to collect the Lewis Guns, as the Coys. are
                   relieved.

6. DEFENSIVE   O. C. D. Coy. will arrange to have defensive
   PATROLS.   patrols out during the relief and withdrawn on
                   completion.

7. MARCH   Distances of 100 yards between platoons will be
   DISCIPLINE.   maintained on the march to LOKE area.

8. RELIEF.   ~~Completion of relief will be reported to Bn.H.Q.
                   by telephone. CODE WORD "DRY"~~

9. Bn.H.Q.   Present Bn.H.Q. will close on completion of relief
                   and reopen at TATINGHEM on arrival.

10. COOKS.   All Cooks at present with Coys. and Bn.H.Q. will
                   proceed to LOKE Area tomorrow morning at 4.30am.
                   A limber will be at the ration dump at that time
                   to take cooking utensils etc. Lieut. Hooley M.C.
                   will be in charge of this party and will arrange
                   that a hot meal is ready for the Battalion when
                   it arrives.

~~11. PETROL, OIL, etc.~~

8. RELIEF.   Completion of relief will be reported to Bn H Qrs
                   by Officers in person who are remaining behind,
                   with the exception of "D" Coy who will report
                   by telephone the code word "DRY."

                                     (Sgd) T.P. NEWMAN.
                                         Capt. & Adjt.
                                     11th Bn. "The Queen's" Regt"

Distribution :-
     Copy No. 1. C.O.   Copy No. 8. Q.M.
            2. Adjt.   9. S.O. & I.O.
            3. O.C. A.Coy.   10. R.S.M.
            4. O.C. B. "   11. War Diary.
            5. O.C. C. "   12. File.
            6. O.C. D. "   13. O/C.2/4th Queen's
            7. 125rd Inf. Bde.   14. Lt. Hooley. M.C.

Adjt.

S E C R E T.   Copy No. 2

ADDENDUM TO OPERATION ORDER No. 26
dated 28th August 1918.

Issued to all recipients of O.Os. No. 26.

1. DELETION.	Delete Para. 10.
2. TRANSPORT.	Two G.S. wagons will be at the disposal of the Battn. on night of 29th inst. for the purpose of taking down all kits, cooking utensils and rations etc. O.C. B. Coy. will detail a guide to meet these wagons at Bde.H.Q. at 9.45 pm and conduct them to the ration dump.
3. COOKING ARRANGEMENTS.	One Cook per Coy. and Bn.H.Q. will report to Lieut. Hooley.M.C. at COMPANY COTTAGE at 4pm today and will proceed to LOYE Area to make arrangements for a hot meal for the Battalion when it arrives. Os. C. Coys. will arrange that the rations for the 30th inst. are withdrawn and packed in sandbags and clearly labelled, together with the cooking utensils will be at the ration dump by 9.45pm. tonight. and loaded on the G.S. wagons and sent to entraining point, the of the cooks will accompany the wagons.
4. GUIDES"	2 N.C.Os. of A. Coy. and 1 N.C.O. of B. & C. Coy will report to Lieut. Hooley. M.C. at COMPANY

COTTAGE at 4pm today to act as guides.

(Sgd) T.P.NEWMAN.
Capt. & Adjt.
11th Bn. "The Queen's" Regt.

11 R W Surrey Rgt
SR 29
123/41

Army Form C. 2118.

WAR DIARY
or
INTELLIGENCE SUMMARY.
(Erase heading not required.)

SEPTEMBER 1918.

Place	Date	Hour	Summary of Events and Information	Remarks and references to Appendices
TATINGHEM	31st Aug		The Battalion awaits the day to cleaning up and reorganising platoon Sections etc. Warning Order received from Bde H.Q. at 10.45 p.m. to the effect that the Battalion would move on the 1st Sept. Transport to start on the 1st by road.	
"	1st Sept		The Battalion Paraded for Divine Service at 11.45 a.m. Remainder of day continued. Operation Orders regarding move were received at 10.45 a.m. Transport moved off at 12 noon, by march route to ABEELE.	
"	2nd "		Battalion were inspected in "Battle Order" by the Commanding Officer at 11.30 a.m. Parades and Bathing off at 3.10 p.m. and marched to ST OMER Station where it entrained at 5 p.m. and proceeded to ABEELE and Battn. arrived at 4.10 p.m. Battalion had tea and then marched to Rebels in 2/G.30.C. on Brit Census Sheet Belgium 5/40 R.Rutways. Billeting being completed at 10.45 p.m. 122nd & 124th Inf Bdes proceeded to front line and relieved the 29th Division.	
POPERINGHE	3rd "		The Battalion spent the day at training etc, and received operation	

WAR DIARY
or
INTELLIGENCE SUMMARY.
(Erase heading not required.)

Army Form C. 2118.

Place	Date	Hour	Summary of Events and Information	Remarks and references to Appendices
	3rd		Operation Orders regarding the Battalions being carried and on 4th inst. but the 12th & 13th Bns. received. Battn. Orders was issued to reserve by from 6 am. 4th inst.	See O.O.
PEPERINGHE	4th		Training carried out by Coys during the morning, and afternoon recreational training. Batt. at 1 hours notice. Warning orders for the move forward received at 9.30 pm.	
"	5th		Training was carried out until 12 noon. Coys preparing to move forward during the afternoon. Battalion moved off at 8.30 pm. to Right Support Positions.	O.Os.
	6th		Battalion in position in Support Area, Right Sub-Sector, at 3-30 am. – disposed between BIERSTRAAT line of Resistance and a line running parallel 500 yds. N.W. of. Bn. HQ. N.15.6.1.8. "C" Coy Right Front, "D" Coy Left Front, "A" Coy Right Rear, "B" Coy Left Rear. Coys working on positions during the day.	
	7th		Sect. Boundary changed – now positions on left reconnoitred. Battalion side-stepped at dusk. Coys disposed in line in the area between a line running through ARTILLERY FARM and N.11.C.4.2 and a line running through ENTERM FARM and N.11.6.9. Bn. HQ. at ARTILLERY FARM.	

WAR DIARY or INTELLIGENCE SUMMARY

Army Form C. 2118.

Place	Date	Hour	Summary of Events and Information	Remarks and references to Appendices
	8/1.		Move completed at 3 a.m. Coys. working on positions all day – improving accommodation etc. Advance party sent up to front line. Front quiet.	
	9/1.		Coys. working on positions during the morning – resting in the afternoon. Commenced relief of 23rd Middx. Regt. in front line Right Sub Sector at 8-30 p.m. Casualties:- 2/Lt. Burchett Wounded.	
	10/1.		Relief completed at 3-15 a.m. Coys disposed as follows:- "B" Coy. Right Front, "D" Coy. Left Front, "C" Coy. Right Support, "A" Coy. Left Support. Bn. H.Q. at N.H.C.8.1. "C" and "A" Coys. working on improving positions during the day. "B" and "D" Coys. working on positions at night with R.E. supervision. Duckboards out up to Front Line Posts at night. Patrols active.	
	11/1.		"C" and "A" Coys. working on positions during the day. "C" Coy. H.Q. shelled early morning. Inter-Company Relief commenced at 10 p.m. "C" Coy. relieved "B" Coy, "A" Coy. relieved "D" Coy. Work carried out on Front Line Posts. Patrols active. Casualties:- Killed; 1 O.R.: Wounded; 2 O.Rs.	
	12/1.		Relief completed at 3 a.m. "B" and "D" Coys. working on positions during the day. "A" and "C" Coys. working on positions at night under R.E. Supervision. 1 Coy. of 10th Bn. The Queen's (R.W.S.) Regt. working on front line posts and carrying material forward. Casualties:- Wounded; 2 O.Rs.	
	13/1.		Support Coys. improving positions by day. Inter-Coy. Relief commenced at night. "B" Coy. relieved "C" Coy. Right Front, "D" Coy. relieved "A" Coy. Left Front. R.Es. and 2 Coys. 10th R.W.Kent Regt. working on front line posts and forward dumps during the night. Casualties:- Wounded; 2 O.Rs.	

Army Form C. 2118.

WAR DIARY
or
INTELLIGENCE SUMMARY.
(Erase heading not required.)

Instructions regarding War Diaries and Intelligence Summaries are contained in F.S. Regs., Part II. and the Staff Manual respectively. Title pages will be prepared in manuscript.

Place	Date	Hour	Summary of Events and Information	Remarks and references to Appendices
	14th		Relief completed at 2.45am. "A" and "C" Coys improving positions during the day. Advance Party went down to take over billets from 26th Bn. Royal Fusiliers in G.23.b. Relief by 18th K.R.R.C. commenced at 9pm. Lieut. Col. W.L. OWEN. M.C. proceeded to GKHATHAM, England, for 4 days course. Major V. HOLDEN. D.S.O, M.C. assumed command.	
	15th		Relief completed at 2 am. Battalion moved to billets in Support Area G.23.b. vacated by 26th Bn. Royal Fusiliers. Baths and cleaning up.	
	16th		Battalion on working party, burying cable for Hot Div. Signal Coy, from 8am to 3pm. Cleaning up for rest of day. 1 OR accidentally wounded.	
	17th		100 ORs on working party constructing A.D.S. Training carried out by remainder of Battalion.	
	18th		Battalion on working party - burying cable. Advance party to new area G.26.	
	19th		100 ORs on working party constructing A.D.S. Remainder training and packing up. Battalion moved off at 1pm by march route to new Support Area G.26. Bn. H.Q. located at G.26.c.5.9.	
	20th		Preparing for Demonstration Scheme.	
	21st		Training during morning - Demonstration Scheme during afternoon.	
	22nd		Baths and Games.	

Army Form C. 2118.

WAR DIARY
or
INTELLIGENCE SUMMARY.
(Erase heading not required.)

Instructions regarding War Diaries and Intelligence Summaries are contained in F. S. Regs., Part II. and the Staff Manual respectively. Title pages will be prepared in manuscript.

Place	Date	Hour	Summary of Events and Information	Remarks and references to Appendices
	23rd		Training under Coy arrangements. Visit from G.O.C. 41st Division.	
	24th.		Training under Coy arrangements.	
	25th.		Brigade Scheme postponed. Training under Coy. arrangements.	
	26th.		Brigade Scheme during afternoon. Battalion in Brigade Reserve.	
	27th.		Battalion rested during this day and paraded at 4.15 p.m. and marched to Dominion Camp reaching there at 11.45 p.m. Orders received at 9.30 a.m. regarding the Operations commencing on 28th.	
PULSE FARM. VOORMEZEELE. KLIEN ZILLEBEKE.	28th		Battalion paraded at 9 a.m. and moved forward to PULSE FARM Hutts Area, where it was situated until 11.15 am when it moved to the RAVINE 2000 yds E of VOORMEZEELE. At 4.45 p.m. it again moved forward to KLIEN ZILLEBEKE when it halted for the night. The CO (Major V. Holden D.S.O. M.C.) attended a conference at Bde H.Q. at 12 noon.	
WERVICQ COMINES RAILWAY.	29th		At 2.6 a.m. orders were received that the 12/3 "Bde would attack at 7.30 a.m. with Middlesex Regt on the right and R.W. Kent Regt on the left with 11th Queens in support, and make good the WERVICQ - COMINES railway. The Battalion moved off at 5.30 a.m. and advanced on line P.15 central - P.20 central - P.20 central where it consolidated its position in Support. Considerable M.G. + Shell fire was encountered otherwise not much opposition. During the afternoon the leading Battalions had to fall back owing to casualties + exposed flanks.	

Army Form C. 2118.

WAR DIARY
or
INTELLIGENCE SUMMARY.
(Erase heading not required.)

Place	Date	Hour	Summary of Events and Information	Remarks and references to Appendices
	29th		The support line then became the front line. This was reorganized and held during the night. Capt. Hopkinson & 16 other ranks wounded.	
	30th		Enemy fairly quiet during the morning. During the afternoon the 12th K.R. Bde relieved the Bde by passing through him, and Battalion remained in their positions.	

R. Newman Lieut Col.
Commanding 11th (S) Bn. "The Queens" (R.W.S.) Regt.

SECRET   C.O.   Copy No. 1.

11th Bn. "The Queen's" Operation Order No. 30

Ref. Map. Sheet 28. S.W.   8th Sept. 1918.

INTENTION. 1. The Battn. will relieve the 23rd Middx. Regt. in the Right Sub-Sector on the night of 9th/10th. inst. On completion of relief the 23rd Middx. Regt. will move back to the positions at present occupied by this Battalion.

DETAIL. 2 (a) Relief

B. Coy 11th Queens will relieve B. Coy 23rd Mdx. Right front.
D. "   "   "   "   " D. "   "   Left "
C. "   "   "   "   " C. "   "   Right Support
A. "   "   "   "   " A. "   "   Left "

2 Platoons of A. Coy will be under the command of O.C. D. Coy for counter attack purposes.

(b) Advance Parties. 1 Officer per Coy and 1 N.C.O. per platoon from B. and D. Coys and 1 N.C.O per the two platoons of A Coy to be attached to D. Coy will report to O.C. 23rd Middx. Regt at 18-30pm tonight. Later they will proceed up the line and

(2).

take over from their opposite numbers.
A Corresponding number from the 23rd Middx
Regt will report at these Headquarters at
3pm 9th inst. They will reconnoitre the
area they will take over and later join
their opposite numbers and guide them
up the line at night.

(c) Guides. Guides for O.C. B. and D. Coys will
be at 23rd Middx H.Q. at 11am 9th inst.

(d) Personnel remaining behind. O.C. Coys will
detail 1 N.C.O. to remain at Coy. H.Q. 24
hours after relief.
1 Officer per Coy. and 1 N.C.O per platoon of
the 23rd Middx. Regt will remain in the line
24 hours after relief.

(e) Details regarding Advance Parties, guides
and moving off etc. for C. Coy and the two
remaining platoons of A. Coy will be arranged
by Coy Comdrs concerned.

(f) Moving off. D. Coy will move off at 8-30pm.
and B. Coy at 8-45pm, platoons at 100
yards intervals.

RATIONS 3. Rations will be at the dump by 6-30pm.
Ration parties will report to Sgt Sparrow

Secret. C.O.   Copy No. 1

Addendum to O.O.30.

9th Sept. 1918.

Ref. "DETAIL" Para 2.(a)

A. Coy. will not send forward two platoons. One only will be sent forward to occupy Counter Attack Position around the Left Coy. H.Q.

The other platoon of A. Coy. will be on the NIERSTRAAT SWITCH Position with the rest of the Coy. (Left Counter Attack Coy.).

(Sd) C.H. Browhead
2/Lieut. & a/Adjt.
11th Bn. 'The Queen's'(R.W.S.) Regt.

Issued to all recipients of O.O. 30.
Issued to Signals at

Secret   Copy No.
1st Bn. "The Queen's" Operation Orders No. 52

Ref. Map Sheet 28 S.W.   10th Sept. 1916

INTENTION   1. Inter-Company Relief on the night 11th/12th inst.

DETAIL   2(a) C. Coy will relieve B. Coy Right Front.
               A. "   "   "Coy" D. "   Left   "
               On completion of B and D Coys will move
               back into positions vacated by C
               and A Coys respectively.
          (b) All details of relief will be arranged
              between Coy Comdrs concerned. The
              usual Advance Parties will be
              exchanged and personnel will be
              left behind 24 hours after relief.
          (c) Moving off. Relief will commence as
              soon as C. and A. Coys have
              drawn rations.

RATIONS 3. C and B Coys' rations will be dumped
             at Right Support Coy Dump.
             A and D Coys' rations will be dumped
             at Left Support Coy Dump.

(2)

Guards for B and D Coys' rations will be arranged by Coy. Comdrs concerned.

TRENCH STORES 4. All trench stores, S.A.A. etc, information and trench maps will be handed over, receipts obtained and duplicates forwarded to Bn. H.Q. by 11 pm 12th inst.

OVER-COATS 5.(a) C and A Coys will collect all over-coats on the 11th inst. They will be rolled and tied in Section bundles, labelled and sent to transport by returning ration limbers.

(b) The Quartermaster will arrange to dump B and D Coys' overcoats at the respective dumps tomorrow's night 11th inst.

REPORT 6. Completion of relief to be reported by wiring the Code word "COT."

7. ACKNOWLEDGE

(Sd) CH Brownhead
2/Lieut & a/Adjt
11th Bn. The Queens Regt.

(3)

Issued to Signals at

Copy No. 1   -   C.O.
"   " 2   -   123rd Inf Bde
"   " 3   -   O.C. A. Coy
"   " 4   -   "   B. "
"   " 5   -   "   C. "
"   " 6   -   "   D. "
"   " 7   -   " H.Q. Coy
"   " 8   -   Quarter Master
"   " 9   -   F.O.
"   " 10   -   War Diary
"   " 11   -   File

SECRET   Copy No. 1
    11th Bn "Queen's" Operation Orders No 33

Ref Map. Sheet 28   Sept. 10th 1918

Intention (1) (a) Dispositions of Left Support Coy will be reorganized.
(b) Present positions occupied by A Coy will be taken over by 23rd Middlesex on the night 12/13th.

Details (2) (a) Left Support Coy will be disposed in the line of resistance between the junction of the line of resistance & the VIERSTRAAT-HALLEBAST Road to the left boundary of the battalion.
(b) O.C. A Coy will make a reconnaissance as soon as possible & commence work on positions decided upon with the least possible delay.
(c) The new positions will be occupied on the night 11/12th by the relieving Coy, if possible though O.C. A Coy will move tonight 10/11th inst.
(d) 23rd Middlesex will commence work on "A Coy's present position tonight.

(2)

Report (3) O.C. A Coy will report his decission after the reckonnaissance.

(sgd) C.H. Brownhead
Lieut & Adjt
11th "Queen's" Regt

Issued to Signals at

Copy No. 1 C.O
 "   " 2 123 Bde.
 "   " 3 A Coy
 "   " 4 B "
 "   " 5 C "
 "   " 6 D "
 "   " 7 23rd Middx Regt.
 "   " 8 War Diary
 "   " 9 File.

(3).

at this hour at the dump

TRENCH STORES 4. All trench stores, S.A.A., bombs, information and trench maps etc will be taken over and a duplicate of the receipt forwarded to this office by 11pm 10th inst.

DRESS. 5. B. and D. Coys will collect all great coats tomorrow 9th inst. They will be rolled and tied in section bundles, labelled clearly and taken to the dump by ration party.

DISPOSITION MAP. 6. A disposition map will be forwarded to Bn. H.Q. by 11pm 10th inst.

COMPLETION OF RELIEF 7. Completion of relief will be reported by wiring the code word "PRESS" and confirmed by runner.

BATT. H.Q. 8. Battn H.Q. will close here at 8-30pm and open at the same time at N.4.c.8.1.

(Sd) C.H. Bromhead
2/Lieut & A/Adjt
11th Bn. "The Queens" Regt.

Issued to Signals at

(4)

DISTRIBUTION

Copy No. 1. — C.O.
" " 2. — 123rd Inf Bde
" " 3. — O.C. A. Coy
" " 4. — O.C. B. "
" " 5. — O.C. C. "
" " 6. — O.C. D. "
" " 7. — Q.M.
" " 8. — S.O. MO & TO
" " 9. — M.O. 23rd Middx Regt
" " 10. — R.S.M.
" " 11. — War Diary
" " 12. — File

SECRET

Copy No. 1.

11th Queen's Operation Order No. 31

Sept 10th 1918.

Intention (1) Inter. Platoon Reliefs

Detail. (2) Coy. Commanders will arrange to relieve front line posts every 24 hours.

Reports. (3) Completion of each relief will be reported by wiring the code word "PLAT".

(sgd) C.H. Bromhead
Lieut/Col
11th Queen's R.W.S. Regt

Copy No. 1. C.O
" " 2. 123rd Bde
" " 3. O.C. A Coy   7. War Diary
" " 4. " B "   8. File
" " 5. " C "
" " 6. " D "

SECRET   Copy No. 1.

11th Queen's Operation Order No. 34.

Ref. Map Sheet 28 S.W.   Sept 12th 1918.

Intention (1) Inter Coy Relief on the night 13/14th.

Detail (2) (a) B Coy will relieve C Coy Right Front
                  D "   "   "   A "   Left   "
On completion of relief C & A Coys will move back into positions vacated by B & D Coys respectively.

(b) All details of relief will be arranged between Coy Commanders concerned.

(c) Relief will commence in the case of B Coy as soon as rations have been drawn & in the case of D Coy, as early as possible.

Rations (3) B Coy. Rations will be dumped as early as possible at Right Support Coy Dump.
D Coy rations will be dumped at Left Front Coy dump at 10.30 p.m.
C Coy rations will be dumped at Right Support Coy dump at 1 a.m.
A Coy rations will be dumped at Left Support Coy dump at 1 a.m.

Trench Stores (4). All Trench Stores, S.A.A. etc, information & trench maps will be handed over, receipts obtained & duplicates forwarded to Bn. H.Q. by 11 p.m. 14th inst.

Overcoats. (5) (a) B & D Coys will collect all overcoats on the 13th inst. They will be

(2)

rolled & tied in section bundles, labled & Sent to Transport by returning ration limbers.

(b) The Quartermaster will arrange to dump C & A Coys overcoats at their respective dumps on the 13th inst with rations.

<u>Completion of Relief</u> (6) Completion of Relief will be reported by wiring the code word "MARR".

(7) Acknowledge.

(sgd) C.H. Bromhead.
Lieut. & Adjt.
11th "Queen's" Regt.

<u>Issued to Signals at</u>

Copy No 1.	C.O.	7. O.C. HQ Coy.
" " 2.	123rd Inf. Bde.	8. Qr. Mr.
" " 3.	OC A Coy	9. I.O.
" " 4.	" B "	10. War Diary.
" " 5.	" C "	11. File.
" " 6.	" D "	

C.O.

Ref O.O. N° 35 dt. 13/9/18

(1) Order of march for the incoming unit will be :- D. A. C. B Coys.

(2) Advance parties from incoming unit will be as follows -
    1 Off. & 1 N.C.O. per Bn HQ
    2 runners " " "
    1 Off. & 1 NCO per Coy HQ
    1 NCO per platoon.

(sgd) H Bromhead
Lieut. & Adjt.
11th Queen's Regt

13/9/18

SECRET.   Copy No. 1
   11th Bn. "The Queens" Operation Order No. 35
Ref. Map Sheet 28   Sept 13th 1918

Intention. (1). The Battn will be relieved by
   the 18th K.R.R.C. on the night 14/15th inst.
   On completion of relief the Bn. will move
   back to support positions at present occupied
   by the 26th R. Fusiliers in G.24.b.
Detail (2) (a) Relief.
A Coy K.R.R. will relieve B Coy 11th Queen's Right Front.
D "   "   "   "   "   D "   "   "   Left   "
B "   "   "   "   "   C "   "   "   Right Support
C "   "   "   "   "   A "   "   "   Left   "
   (b) Advance Parties. 1 officer per Coy, 1 N.C.O
   per platoon + 1 officer + 1 N.C.O. per Bn H.Q
   will report at Bn H.Q. at 2 pm. tomorrow
   14th inst. Later they will proceed to the
   Support Area in G.24.b. + take over billets
   from their opposite Nos of the 26th R. Fusiliers.
   Instructions for meeting the Bn. will be
   issued later. The Offrs + N.CO's from B.+D. Coys
   will be accommodated at Bn H.Q. tomorrow
   14th inst. A Corresponding Advance Party from
   the 18th K.R.R.C. will report at Bn H.Q. tonight
   at 8.30 pm. Later they will be guided to
   the units they are relieving.
   (c) Guides:- Guides to meet the incoming
   unit will be supplied as follows:—

(2)

B & D Coys — 1 per platoon & 1 per Coy H.Q.
C " — 1 each per 2 platoons only & 1 per Coy H.Q.
A " — 1 each " 3 " " & 1 " " "

These guides will be on the road outside Bn H.Q. at 8.15 p.m. on the 14th inst. Coy Commanders will ensure that their guides receive full instructions.

C & A Coys are only supplying 3 & 4 guides respectively owing to the relieving Coys only consisting of 2 & 3 platoons respectively.

B & D Coys guides will report to Bn H.Q. before dawn 14th inst. where they will be accommodated for the day.

(d) Personnel remaining behind. 1 officer per Coy & 1 N.C.O. per platoon will remain in the line until dawn on the 15th inst. The S.O. will arrange to send back a cyclist runner to guide this personnel to the new area. He will wait for them at Bn H.Q.

(e) Moving off. Distance of at least 100 yds between platoons to be maintained.

Rations (3) The Quartermaster will arrange to dump rations in the new area & have a hot meal ready for the time of arrival.

Overcoats (4) B & D Coys overcoats will be dumped in the new area. C & A Coys will collect overcoats on the 14th inst. They w

(3)

be rolled, & tied in section bundles & dumped at their respective section dumps. The Transport Officer will arrange to collect these as soon as possible.

<u>Transport.</u> (5) Lewis Gun Limbers for B & D Coys will be at a point 100 yds W. of Bn HQ. at 12.30 a.m.

Lewis Gun Limbers afor C & A Coys will be at their respective dumps at 11 p.m.

One limber will report to Bn HQ. at 7 p.m. & another at 10 p.m.

<u>Trench Stores.</u> (6) All trench stores, information obtained by patrol, trench maps, programmes of work etc. will be handed over, receipts obtained & duplicates forwarded to Bn HQ.

<u>Completion of Relief.</u> (7) Completion of Relief will be reported by wiring the code word "MAN".

<u>Bn HQrs.</u> (8) Bn HQ will close here on completion of relief & open in the new area at the same hour.

(9) Acknowledge

(Sgd.) C N Bromhead
Lieut & Adjt.
11th Queen's (R.W.S.) Regt

Issued to Sigs at.

Copy No 1. CO   5. OC C Coy   9 MO, LGO & IO
" " 2. 123 Inf Bde.   6. " D "   10 18th K.R.R.C.
" " 3. OC A Coy   7. T.O & Q.M.   11. War Diary
" " 4. " B "   8. OC H.Q. Coy 12 File.

SECRET.   Copy No. 3

OPERATION ORDER No.36.
11th Bn.   "The Queen's" Regt.

Ref. Map Sheet 28.   1/40,000.   September 18th 1918.

INTENTION.   1. The Battalion will move into billets in Support
                     Area G.36. tomorrow, the 19th instant.

DETAIL.   2.(a). Advance Party. One complete section per
                     Company and 1 N.C.O. and 6 men per Battn.
                     H.Q. will proceed to the new area to-night
                     and prepare the billets for occupation. They
                     will report to Lieut. C.C. Prescott on
                     arrival for instructions.
                  (b). Order of March. Battn. H.Q. B, C, D. and
                     A. Coys. Intervals of 50 yards between
                     Companies will be maintained.
                  (c). Parade. The Battn. will parade in column
                     of route on the football field at 1pm.
                     Head of column facing N.
                  (d). Route.   Cross Roads G.25c.7.4.
                                      "   G.33.b.6.4.
                                      "   G.27.d.8.6.
                  (e). Guides. Guides will meet the Battn. at
                     Cross Roads G.27.d.8.6. at 1.45p.m.
                     They will also meet the working party at the
                     same place at 4.30 p.m.
                  (f). Baggage. Officers' valises and packs of men
                     on working party and stores etc. will be
                     stacked in a convenient place for transport
                     by 10 a.m.
                     Stretchers to be dumped outside R.A.P. by 11 am.

TRANSPORT.   3. Two G.S. Wagons for baggage will report to
                     Battn. H.Q. about 10 a.m.
                     L.G. Limbers will report to their respective
                     Coys. at 11 a.m. They will remain move off with
                     their respective Companies.
                     The Mess Cart will collect Mess kit at
                     12.30 p.m. The Maltese Cart will report to
                     the R.A.P. at 12p.m.

REPORTS.   4. All reports to the head of the column.

BATTN. H.Q.   5. Battn. H.Q. will close here at 1 p.m. and open
                     at the same hour at G.36.c.5.9.

                                         (Sgd) C.H. BROWNHEAD
                                         2/Lieut. & A/Adjt.
                                         11th Bn.   "The Queen's" Regt.

Issued to Signals at :-

        Copy No.1. C.O.   8. Q.M. & T.O.
             2. 123rd Inf. Bde.   9. Lieut. Prescott.
             3. Adjt.   10. M.O. & L.G.O.
             4. O.C. A. Coy.   11. R.S.M.
             5. " B. "   12. File.
             6. " C. "   13. War Diary.
             7. " D. "   14. Spare.

Operation Order.
11th Bn "The Queen's Regt"
                                        Copy
Ref Map Sheet 29.   24th October 1918
1.
INTENTION.   The 41st Division will
            resume the attack on 25th October.
Intermed. Objective — L'ESCAUT.
Objective. The 123rd Inf. Bde will attack with
P25.b.90.95 the 23rd Bn Mdx Regt on the right
to P26.d.1.3 and 11th Bn "The Queen's Regt" on the
            left.
    2.   Zero hour — 0904
DETAIL   In accordance with the above the
         Battalion will carry out the
         attack as follows:—
         "A" Coy — Right Front Coy plus
         1 Machine Gun, Frontage as
         shewn on Coy Map.
         "C" Coy — Left Front Coy, frontage
         as shewn on Coy Map.
         "B" Coy — Left Support Coy plus
         Battalion Scouts, 1 M. Gun, and
         1 Stokes Mortar Gun.

"A" Coy 10th R.W.Kents, mopped up. ~~plus 1 M.Gun.~~ Coy HQ Oso plus 1 Platoon will follows right front Coy. 1 M.Gun will go with this party.

1 Platoon will follow Left Support Coy.

"D" Coy — Reserve Coy — plus one M.Gun. They will occupy a position at about O.17.c.70.90. and will not move without direct orders from Bn. H.Q.

※

3. One 18 pr Gun will be attached to the Battalion and will take up position on the road at 17.a. ~~45.55~~ 70.30.

In the event of Coy Comdrs meeting with strong opposition at any particular point, they will immediately call upon Bn H.Q. for the help of this gun ~~as soon after zero as possible~~

4. One Section of D Coy 10th M.G.C. will be at the disposal of the Battalion. At 3am they will be located at 17b 10.10. At Zero plus 30 they will occupy positions in the houses between 17d 20.80 and 17a 55.90. From these houses they will give the attacking coys as much support as possible, dealing with overhead fire with enemy M.Gs. and with any opposition which is possible to engage. As soon as the Red Line is reached this Section goes into Bde Reserve.

5. SPECIAL SIGNAL.

In the event of a Strong point holding out against attacking Coys or Mopping Up, the Platoon or Coy Cmdr concerned will fire a white Very Light at the point from which the opposition comes. Battalion Observers will be on the look out for these signals, it must be understood that this does not in any way relieve the attacking troops of their responsibilities.

✳ ~~After~~ As soon as the final objective is reached A Coy R W Kent Reg' will concentrate at P.32.d.45.90.

6 CONTACT AEROPLANE
A Contact aeroplane will fly over the area at 10.30 a.m. and 11.30 a.m. All ranks will be warned of this and Section & Platoon Leaders will be specially shew their areas by light flares.

7 CONSOLIDATION
On arrival at the final objective the position will be consolidated in depth. Patrols will be pushed forward to cover any

bridgehead that may exist.

7. Synchronization of watches will take place at 12 M N at present Bn H.Q. and again at Bn Battle H.Q. at 017a 40.30 at 6 am.

(8) Coys will commence to get into position at 2 am and they will report to Bn Battle H.Q. when they are in position.

(9) Coys will each send a guide to Bn H.Q. at 4 am to take the M. Guns which are being attached to them.

BARRAGE.
9. The following is the approximate times of Barrage.
Zero minus 4 mins Barrage comes down 200ˣ in front of battle positions

9. At Zero the Barrage moves forward and Infantry advances. At Zero plus 1hr + 25 mins the Barrage reaches the Red line for pause.

At Zero plus 1hr 35 mins Barrage ceases.

At Zero plus 3 hrs 23 mins Barrage opens.

At Zero plus 3 hrs 25 mins Barrage moves forward and Infantry advances.

The rate of the Barrage will be 100 yds per 2 mins, and will pause every 1500 yards for 6 mins.

10. Bn H.Q.
Present H.Q. will close at 3 am and open at O.17.a.40.3. at the same time.

During the pause on the Red Line Bn H.Q. will open on X.do.P.a.9. central.

LIAISON.

Liaison Posts will be established as follows:-
WITH 124 Bde:-
P19a 3.3. P26 b 2.1. P34 a 8.0.9.5.
WITH Mdx Regt:-
O 30 b a.2. Level Crossing at P31a

11. Level Crossing at P32d 9.1
The R.A.P. will be established first at 17a.00.70, later to P25 central.

1st Division A.

123rd.I.B.
G.226/33.

Herewith War Diaries for 123rd.Infantry Brigade and units of the Brigade for month of October 1918.

21st Nov.1918.

Brigadier General.
Commanding 123rd.Infantry Brigade.

11th Queens R.W.Surrey 123/4/1
Army Form C. 2118.
OCTOBER 1918.
Vol 30

WAR DIARY
or
INTELLIGENCE SUMMARY.
(Erase heading not required.)

Place	Date	Hour	Summary of Events and Information	Remarks and references to Appendices
YPRES	Oct/1918 1st		Orders received at 1am. for Bn. to move by road route at 4am. to YPRES - MENIN Rd. via TENBRIELEN and AMERICA. The Battalion moved at 6.35am. On reaching TENBRIELEN the Bn. halted owing to advanced Guards of 22nd Bde. being checked at AMERICA. At 4.25pm. orders were received for the Battalion to attack with 23rd Middlesex on K.right and make good the railway WERVICQ - MENIN. The Battalion assembled on the line at 5.15pm. and advanced at 5.45pm. (C.D. in front. B + A in Support.) After advancing about 1500 yds. it came under very heavy Machine Gun fire from tall chicory fields on Q and came to casualties and darkness it was not possible to go farther, and the Battalion halted and dug in on the line. Casualties - Killed - Capt. Bahn 2/Lieut Shawson. Wounded - 2/Lieut Edwards - 2/Lieuts Denton + Gray. During the march to the place of assembly the Battalion came under very heavy shell fire and sustained casualties were caused. Major Holden D.S.O. M.C. was severely wounded + 2/Lieut. Coates M.C. T.M.B. was killed.	A A A
WERVICQ MENIN R.W.	2nd		The movement forward was made on this date by the Bn. but a local attack was carried out on the left, and an improvement was made in our positions. Situation remained quiet throughout the night.	A
	3rd		Day remained quiet. Snipers became evident throughout the day from a farm on the right flank. Battalion was relieved about 12 midnight by the Argyll + Sutherland Highlanders + moved back to T34 A4.9	A

WAR DIARY or INTELLIGENCE SUMMARY

Army Form C. 2118.

Place	Date	Hour	Summary of Events and Information	Remarks and references to Appendices
	4th		Batt. relieved by elements of the 34th Div: arrived in support area T.35a. at 4.30am After a good rest reorganising and cleaning commenced. Capt Blount (RF) assumed command.	
	5th		Cleaning up and reorganising. Lieut Owen MC returned from leave assumed command 'C' Coy. Reinforcements 2/Lt Williams, Hunt, Jacks & 2/Lt Price. 2 ORs. 28 ORs returned from leave & hospital.	
	6th		Refitting & reorganising. Forward areas reconnoitred. Games in afternoon. Reinforcements 21 ORs. (19 from Corps School).	
	7th		Training and games in morning. Took over support positions from the 10th 12th Bn The Queens in T.35d. in evening.	
	8th		Training, games & reconnoitring forward areas. 1 OR. wounded.	
	9th		Training & reconnoitring etc. Advance parties sent to the line.	
	10th		Games in morning. Relieved 10th R.W.Kents in frontline at night. 1Coy Bathurst attacked. Relief completed 21.20. Front line posts readjusted to straighten line. Our artillery very active.	
	11th		Hostile counter bombardment about 04.30 to 05.45. Our artillery very active during the day. Both sides abnormally quiet at night. A Coy relieved platoon of H.L.I. on left at night so extending front. Patrols active all along our front. Casualties 1 OR. wounded. 2 ORs attd. wounded.	
	12th		Day quiet. 6 ORs. 122 Bde reps in morning. Relieved by 12th East Surreys at night. Relief completed midnight - moved back to Support area T.35a.	

Army Form C. 2118.

WAR DIARY
or
INTELLIGENCE SUMMARY.
(Erase heading not required.)

Instructions regarding War Diaries and Intelligence Summaries are contained in F. S. Regs., Part II. and the Staff Manual respectively. Title pages will be prepared in manuscript.

Place	Date	Hour	Summary of Events and Information	Remarks and references to Appendices
POULTEN FARM	13th		Resting all day.	
	14th		2nd Army attacked 5.35am. Moved off from Support area at 6.35am. Bombardment to POULTEN FARM area Regd. B.H.Q. POULTEN FARM. Reinforcements 6 offs + 144 O.Rs.	
	15th		All day at POULTEN FARM.	
	16th		Marched Lys area, left POULTEN FARM 7.30am. Stores rested in billets 2.17 under 4 hours. March to line + relieved 12 Bn. R.I.R. (36th Div) in left sub sector (COURTRAI) Relief complete 10.30pm.	
COURTRAI	17th		Hostile shelling fair on right 10.30pm. Reconnaissance made of canal bank 18thCanal running fair during the day. Sent section in order to handling crossed the Lys Nth of COURTRAI in an old boat + patrolled enemy side. No opposition at all. all returned safely.	
	18th		Ordered to cross Lys Nth of COURTRAI if possible 11am Bn. H.Q. moved forward followed by C + D Coys. Bn. concentrated He area H20.d21 Hostile M.G. active when first attempt made to cross soon dealt with. B.Coy crossed followed by P. Coy then C. Coy B.Coy pushed forward made good railway from canal to H22d. P. Coy pushed up BOSSUYT Canal dropping flank posts en route. C. Coy pushed forward to railway + reinforced B. Coy.	
	19th		1 post pushed forward at night 200yds. Patrols sent over canal + ammunition. Younsoo taken by B. Coy. Casualties 2/Lt Talbot (T.M.B.) wounded 6 O.Rs wounded 1 O.R. killed.	
BOSSUYT			Died of wounds 2 ORs. (T.M.B.)	

Army Form C. 2118.

WAR DIARY
or
INTELLIGENCE SUMMARY.
(Erase heading not required.)

Instructions regarding War Diaries and Intelligence Summaries are contained in F. S. Regs., Part II. and the Staff Manual respectively. Title pages will be prepared in manuscript.

Place	Date	Hour	Summary of Events and Information	Remarks and references to Appendices
	20th		Relieved at 4am by H.M.Gs. from 29th Div. Moved from Peselems farm through COURTRAI & concentrated in M. area. Troops resting all day.	
	21st		Battalion moved off at 6am. to New area when it was distributed in farms. At 3.30pm it moved into N.18.d. area when it stayed the night.	
	22nd		Battalion remained in N.18.d. area that day. At 12.45pm a warning order was received from Bde. to move. At 4.30pm an order was received to move into O.16.b. + O.17.a area & take up position in Bois Passroil.	
	23rd		Battalion remained in the area O.16 + 17. A certain amount of shelling was experienced during the day.	
	24th		Battalion still remained in reserve but orders were received at 11pm. that it would move up and relieve the R.W. Kents early on morning of 25th and take part in operations on that day.	
	25th		Move completed at 4am. Boys hopped up on Assembling line at 6am. At 9am boys moved forward under a barrage and made rapid progress. At HUSTRIT B.T.C. boys met with stiff resistance but after heavy fighting captured the village. He line that night ran East of HUSTRIT.	
HUSTRIT				
AVILGHEM	26th		Battalion resumed the advance about 10am. AVILGHEM and by 4pm had made good all objectives. Bn. was relieved by 15th Hants. Regt. at dusk, and moved to KNOKKE where it halted for the night. Next day afterwards moved to COURTRAI where it was located in the Barracks.	
KNOKKE				

Army Form C. 2118.

WAR DIARY
or
INTELLIGENCE SUMMARY.
(Erase heading not required.)

Instructions regarding War Diaries and Intelligence Summaries are contained in F. S. Regs., Part II. and the Staff Manual respectively. Title pages will be prepared in manuscript.

Place	Date	Hour	Summary of Events and Information	Remarks and references to Appendices
	27th		Was devoted to clearing up and reorganizing	
	28th		Was devoted to clearing up and reorganizing	
	29th		Was devoted to clearing up and reorganizing	
	30th		Companies paraded and carried out demonstrations in attack &c.	
	31st		Companies paraded and carried out demonstrations in attack &c.	

J.A. Merriman (Copy)
Lieut. Col.
Commanding 11th (S) Bn. The Queen's (R.W.S.) Regt.

WAR DIARY or INTELLIGENCE SUMMARY

11 RW Surrey B
Army Form C. 2118.

Ref. Map. Sheet 5. Tournai.

Place	Date	Hour	Summary of Events and Information	Remarks and references to Appendices
Courtrai	Nov/18 1st		Battalion moved from COURTRAI to the KNOKKE AREA. Arrived at 1.45 p.m. and reached KNOKKE area about 4.20 p.m. Battalion was billeted in scattered farms. The following to E.O. and Men were awarded the Military Medal for gallantry and devotion to duty during the operations near GHELUWE from 28th Sept. to 3rd October 1918. No. 10811 L/Sgt Goldsmith, 6961 Pte Baker, 207067 Cpl Kait, 207954 Sgt Aries (since deceased) 207993 L.C. Littlewood, 8456 L.C. Joyce, 6986 L.S. Bartlett, 6930 L/Cpl King, 40078 Pte Marshall, 22941 L.C. Smith.	
Knokke Area	2nd		Coys practised the attack, especially by platoons, making use of smoke grenades. During afternoon troops played games.	
	3rd		During the morning Coys cleaned up. Church Parade was held at 10.30 a.m. Afternoon was devoted to sports.	
	4th		Orders were received for battalion to relieve D.L.I. (124th Bde) in the front line, and marched off at 1.30 p.m., halting for tea about 1½ miles N.W. of INGOYGHEM. Afterwards marching off and relieved D.L.I. in the BERCHEM sector on the RIVER SCHELDT. Bn. HQrs at Xrds at K in KREYELSTRAAT.	
Berchem	5th		Relief completed at 1.35 a.m. Day quiet, occasional shelling of road junctions. A patrol reconnaitred the river bank with the object of finding, and was successful in locating 3 hostile Machine Guns. Civilian movement reported eastwards.	

WAR DIARY or INTELLIGENCE SUMMARY

Army Form C. 2118.

(Erase heading not required.)

NOVEMBER 1918.   REF. MAP SHEET No 5. TOURNAI.

Place	Date	Hour	Summary of Events and Information	Remarks and references to Appendices
BERCHEM SECTOR	6th	4.00	At 4 am a violent counter preparation was put down by the enemy and caused several small fires in the Battalion area. A daylight patrol under Corpl POWELL M.M. reconnoitred the river bank, and ascertained that the enemy were still occupying the eastern bank. Enemy artillery fairly active on Battn area throughout the day. KERKHOVE receiving considerable attention. TENHOVE was also shelled. At dusk the 18th K.R.'s relieved 'B' Coy in TENHOVE, who moved into support. Casualties 3 O.R. wounded.	
	7th	4 to 6am	From 4 to 6am enemy artillery was very active on Battalion front. At 1am 'C' 'D' Coys cleared all parties noted on their fronts. Enemy movement was observed in MEERSCHE during the day and was dealt with by Lewis Guns. An observation was kept on the river, which was found to be in flood owing to heavy rains. At 8 pm a patrol under the direction of Capt HEDLEY M.C. attempted to cross the SCHELDT in a boat. The boat had been hastily damaged by shell fire, and sank when the first party went across, throwing them into the water; they escaped the remainder and gained the EASTERN bank. The boat was recovered and further attempts were made without success and after a lot of difficulty this an attempt was made by 'C' Coy to cross the river near GRIJKOORT that has to be abandoned on account of heavy machine gun fire which prevented them reaching the river.	
	8th		The following were awarded the MILITARY MEDAL for gallantry & devotion to duty during the crossing of the RIVER LYS on 18th Oct 1918. No 22821 Pte Bellsupp A.E. 12865 Pte W Foster, 11694 Pte L Allison. 2414 Pte G Saunders.	

Army Form C. 2118.

WAR DIARY
or
INTELLIGENCE SUMMARY.
(Erase heading not required.)

Instructions regarding War Diaries and Intelligence Summaries are contained in F. S. Regs., Part II. and the Staff Manual respectively. Title **NOVEMBER 1918.** REF: MAP SHEET No 5. TOURNAI.

Place	Date	Hour	Summary of Events and Information	Remarks and references to Appendices
	8/11		At 1.30 a.m. a patrol visited the point where C Coy. were found to cross the river and observed an enemy sapping party which was engaged by our artillery. Occasional bursts of artillery fire by the enemy took place during the day, including a number of gas shells. A direct hit on Bn Hd Qrs by a gas shell caused one casualty. Two daylight patrols went out along river bank and were fired on by the enemy. It was decided to try and cross the river again as soon as it was dark enough, and after a Conference, a strong patrol under Capt. HEDLEY M.C. was ordered to cross the river at the N. in MEERSCHE and reconnoitre the Village, if no opposition was met with the village to be occupied and patrols pushed out. If opposition was met with the village to be occupied and patrols withdrawn. At this period there were not any indications of an enemy withdrawal. A collapsible canvas boat was procured and a section of Royal Engineers under Lt SHAW R.E. took charge of the operation of getting the patrol across the river. The situation was fairly quiet with the exception of occasional bursts of M.G. fire. The boat was launched and at 9.30 p.m. the crossing commenced. The point was lost paddled across by means of 3 hand this proved very difficult on account of a very strong current however within end of the hour it was accomplished and a rope was secured to the opposite end of the patrol and in order to pull it backward and forward. The crossing of the patrol was complete in two journeys as the boat would only hold 5 men at a time, and the patrol pushed on to the village. At this period very close touch was kept with the French on the left who were attacking the village of the enemy. At 11 pm a message was received from Capt HEDLEY to the effect that he had cleared the village of the enemy. Orders were immediately issued	

Army Form C. 2118.

WAR DIARY
or
INTELLIGENCE SUMMARY.

(Erase heading not required.)

NOVEMBER 1918.   Ref: MAP SHEET No 5 TOURNAI

Place	Date	Hour	Summary of Events and Information	Remarks and references to Appendices
	8th.		For the remainder of the Battalion turned at this time endeavouring to cross the SCHELDT. "C" Coy at KERKHOVE were at this time endeavouring to cross the river at BRITKOORT, but the enemy was very active there, and it was given up. The whole Battalion crossed the river by means of the one boat. (Canadian Pct).	
BERCHEM & MEERSCHE AREA.	9th.		At 12.1 a.m. an order was issued to O.C. "D" Coy (Capt HEDLEY) to push on and make good the AUDENARDE – BERCHEM Railway, at 1.30 a.m. a message was received from the Front Companies to the effect that they were investing in the operation. At 3 a.m. the whole of the Battalion had crossed the river and was established in MEERSCHE. "C" Coy was ordered to push out on the right and send patrols in direction of BERCHEM. This was done, the patrols entering BERCHEM and capturing a prisoner. At 3.50 a.m. patrols were well SOUTH OF Railway, and pushing forward to the high ground near NUKERKE. At 9.15 a.m. an order was received from Bde H.Q. to halt at the line of the railway, but at this time the Front Troops were considerably in front of this line. Patrols were sent out to gain touch on the right and left. Touch was obtained with the French on the left but could not be obtained on the right. The patrols pushing forward met with considerable M.G. fire, and Hallo's at 12.30 the R.W. Kent & 23/Mx relieved the Battn in the outpost line and the Battalion withdrew to MEERSCHE. The total of front which the Battalion held at the commencement of the operation was 1700 yds, and when relieved held a front of 3000 yards.	

D. D. & L., London, E.C.
(A504) Wt. W1771/M1 31 750,000 3/47 Sch 52 Forms/C2118/14

Army Form C. 2118.

WAR DIARY
or
INTELLIGENCE SUMMARY.
(Erase heading not required.)

NOVEMBER 1918.   REF. MAP SHEET No 5. TOURNAI.

Instructions regarding War Diaries and Intelligence Summaries are contained in F. S. Regs., Part II. and the Staff Manual respectively. Title pages will be prepared in manuscript.

Place	Date	Hour	Summary of Events and Information	Remarks and references to Appendices
	9th	6.30 p.m.	At 6.30 p.m. the Battalion moved from MEERSCHE to SUSIQUE, arriving there about 9 p.m., the Battn was billeted in the village.	
	9th/10th	9.30 a.m.	At 9.30 a.m. the Battalion moved from SUSIQUE and marched to SCHOORISSE via NUKERKE++ and reached in farms on the high ground 1½ miles S.E. of SCHOORISSE.	
	11th		Battalion remained in SCHOORISSE Area. At 9.45 a.m. an message was received that the Armistice was signed, and that Hostilities would cease at 11 a.m. and troops would stand fast on the line reached at that hour. No further move was made during the day. Orders were issued prohibiting fraternizing with the enemy.	
	12th		Battalion remained in SCHOORISSE AREA. The following Officers were awarded the MILITARY CROSS for Operations during period 28th to 4th (Copy att) T.P. Newman Capt, R.T. Edwards 2/Lt, E. Mann 2/Lt (Sence Edwards)	
	13th		At 7 a.m. Battalion moved forward to Outpost Line at BRAMMONT relieving the L.N. Lancs 31st Divn. Dispositions — "A" & "C" Coys in Outpost Line, "B" & "D" Coys in Support in GEOFFERDINGHE. Relief Completed at 2.30 p.m.	
	14th		Battalion remained in same area. Coys spent the day in refitting and cleaning up. Warning Order received that Divison would be moving forward to the German Frontier in a few days.	
	15th		Cleaning up, etc, continued. Inter Coy relief carried out "B" relieving "A" and "D" relieving "C" Coy.	

Army Form C. 2118.

WAR DIARY
or
INTELLIGENCE SUMMARY.

NOVEMBER 1918. REF. MAP SHEETS. 5 & 6 TOURNAI. + BRUSSELS

Place	Date	Hour	Summary of Events and Information	Remarks and references to Appendices
FROIDEPONCHE	16th		"A" Coy was relieved by 23rd Man. Regt and "D" Coy moved further to the right relieving 2nd Leinster Regt. Clearing up etc. continued. (also "D" Coy) was inspected, and afterwards lectures by the Coma. Officer on march discipline etc. Orders received for move forward.	
	17th		The Battalion Paraded ready to move off at 7am. Order of March. H.Q.Drs, A.B.C.D. Transport; — Route:— SARALDINGHE — PLANKEN — LES DEUX ACREN, to HERRINNES. Battn arrived about 2pm, and were billeted in the Town.	
HERRINNES	18th			
	19th		Battalion remained in HERRINNES.	
	20th		At 2am Orders were received that the Division would be relieved that day by another Division, and 123rd Bde Comp. would move back to LES DEUX ACREN — GHOY Area. Battalion paraded and moved off at 8.30 am — Order of March, Bn HQ — B.C.D.A. Transport. Route VIANE — LES DEUX ACREN. Battn reaches billets in STAROY about 2.15pm.	
STAROY	21st		Battalion remained in same Area. Clearing up & fitting of equipment was carried out. Afternoon was devoted to Sports.	

Army Form C. 2118.

WAR DIARY
or
INTELLIGENCE SUMMARY.

(Erase heading not required.)

NOVEMBER 1918. REF: MAP SHEET. 5 TOURNAI.

Instructions regarding War Diaries and Intelligence Summaries are contained in F. S. Regs., Part II. and the Staff Manual respectively. Title pages will be prepared in manuscript.

Place	Date	Hour	Summary of Events and Information	Remarks and references to Appendices
	22nd		Battalion remains in same area. Coys parades tender their own arrangements. Afternoon was devoted to sports. Education Committee details to see the Education of Battn. Lieut. CHINN was nominated as President.	
	23rd		Coys parades under their own arrangements. Afternoon was devoted to sport. Lieut. L.G. MAWKING was awarded the MILITARY CROSS for gallantry & devotion to duty during the operation of crossing the L'ys on 18th October 1918.	
	24th		Open Air Memorial Parade was held at 10:15 a.m. Coys practised Marched past, etc. At 11:30 a.m. Church Parade was held. Afternoon was devoted to Sports.	
	25th		A Composite Company composed of one Platoon from each Coy, representing the Battn. in the Bde Parade when a distribution of medal ribbons to the following:- under Command of Capt C.J.M. 1918 MC M.C. Capt + Adjt F.P. Newman DCM. Lieut E.W.J. Newn. Lieut L.G. Mawking. M.M. 10811 C.S.M. Holdsworth. 6986 Sgt Bartlett. 22891 Sgt Batcup 7456 L/Cpl Joyce, 12865 Pte Foote. The Company afterwards marched past the Divisional Commander. Afternoon was devoted to games.	

Army Form C. 2118.

WAR DIARY
or
INTELLIGENCE SUMMARY.
(Erase heading not required.) REF: MAP SHEET No 6. TOURNAI

NOVEMBER 1918.

Place	Date	Hour	Summary of Events and Information	Remarks and references to Appendices
TOOOT	26th		Companies paraded from 9am to 12 noon. Afternoon was devoted to Games.	
	27th		Companies paraded from 9am to 12 noon. Afternoon devoted to games. "B" Coy played "D" Coy M.G.C in Divl Football Competition & lost 3-1.	
	29th		Bat Cross Country run off. The 1st Prize in Divl Cross Country Run was obtained by "D" Coy's team. Score 229. "D" Coy played A/190 R.F.A in Divl Football Competition & won 4-3.	
	30th		Battalion Paraded at 10am for Batta Drill under the Coy Officers. Afternoon - "A" Coy played "D" Coy 23/Middx in Divl. Football Competition. 2nd Round & lost 5-0. "D" Coy played A/190 R.F.A in 3rd Round - Result 1-1.	

30th Nov 1918.

W. Owen Lieut Colonel
Commdg 11th Bn The Queens Regt

C.O.

Special Order No 1
by
Lieut Col W.L Owen M.C. Commanding 11th Bn Queens
Sunday 17 Nov 1918

No 1 Note
Move

The 41st Division will begin its march to the German frontier tomorrow 18th inst.

2/ Parade

The Battn less D. Coy: will parade ready to move off at 8 am.
Starting point. Battn HdQrs facing SARALDINGE.
Order of march. Signallers. Band. Battn HdQrs. A.B.C. Transport.
Route — PLANKEN — LES DEUX ACREN — VIANE.
Destination — GAMMERAGES — FJSBROEK area.
Dress. Fighting Order.
D. Coy. will parade under arrangements made by O.C. D. Coy & will be ready at D. Coy Hd: Qrs: to move at 9 am. and will take its place in the column behind C. Coy as the Battn passes. O.C. D. Coy will withdraw the outposts at 6 am.

3/ Routine

Reveille. 5.30 am. Breakfast 6.30 am. "Orders" 1½ hours after reaching new billets.

4/ Blankets, packs, etc:

Blankets & packs will be stacked outside each Coy. HdQrs ready for loading at 6.30 a.m. Officers valises will be ready for loading at 6.45 a.m. Mess Kits will be ready at 7.15 am.

5/ Billeting Party.

The N.C.O's detailed as billeting party will parade under 2nd Lieut Maudling at Batt Hd Qrs. at 7.15 am. This party will report to the Staff Captain at GRAMMONT railway station at 8 am tomorrow 18th inst

(Sg) T. P. NEWMAN.

Capt & Adjutant
11th Battn The Queens (R.W.S.) Regt

Army Form C. 2118.

11 R W Surrey

WAR DIARY
or
INTELLIGENCE SUMMARY.
(Erase heading not required.)

Instructions regarding War Diaries and Intelligence Summaries are contained in F. S. Regs., Part II. and the Staff Manual respectively. Title pages will be prepared in manuscript.

DECEMBER 1918.   REF: MAP SHEET No 6. TOURNAI.

V 31 3 2

Place	Date	Hour	Summary of Events and Information	Remarks and references to Appendices
	1st		Church Services for Roman Catholics & Non Conformists were held at CHOY. Afternoon was devoted to Sport.	
	2nd		A Ceremonial Parade by the Battalion took place at 10 a.m. Afternoon - 'D' Coy replaced 'A' Coy Piostrents in Gas room Drill Tooth Competition & Foot. 2.O. The following were awarded decorations for conspicuous gallantry in action in crossing the L/S on 18th Oct. 18 and subsequent operations on 23rd & 26th October 1918.	
			DISTINGUISHED SERVICE ORDER - Temp Lieut Colonel W.L. OWEN M.C.	
			A/Capt: C.J.M. PAIGE M.C.	
			BAR TO MILITARY MEDAL. - 11056 Sergt E. QUAIFE M.M. 67861 Pte C. BAKER MM.	
			MILITARY MEDAL. 40039 Pte N. UNDERHILL. 34576 L.C. C. BILLMORE. 1335 Cpl N. STONER. 23085 L.C. W. UNDERHILL. 40045 Pte A. HARDING. 13085 Sgt J. WORSTER. 204949 Cpl G. GREEN. 10826 Sgt H. BUTCHER. 40068 Pte T. ROWNTREE. 18438 L.C. J. DOWLING. 40091 Cpl G. CASTLE. 34204 Pte A. WANLESS.	

STO 005

Army Form C. 2118.

WAR DIARY
or
INTELLIGENCE SUMMARY.
(Erase heading not required.)

Ref: Map Sheet No 5. Tournai

DECEMBER 1918.

Instructions regarding War Diaries and Intelligence Summaries are contained in F.S. Regs., Part II. and the Staff Manual respectively. Title pages will be prepared in manuscript.

Place	Date	Hour	Summary of Events and Information	Remarks and references to Appendices
STODOY	3rd		Owing to weather conditions Boys paraded in Billets, and various inspections held.	
	4th		Coys paraded in Billets owing to weather, and Transport went to Baths. Afternoon, "C" Coy Bn H.Q.	
	5th		"B" "A" & "D" Coys went to Baths. At 11.30am the G.O.C. 123rd Inf Bde (Br General M. Kemp-Welch D.S.O.) inspected "B" & "C" Coys and Regtl Transport. Afternoon - Regt Cross Country Run - Result II Coy Pte 'B' Coy 2nd - Reinforcements arrived - Strength 94.	
	6th		Battalion went on Route March, moved off at 9.30am. Route - STODOY - LESSINES - GRAMMONT ROAD - LESSINES - OST - GHOY - STODOY. Afternoon - Regt Football Match versus 139th Field Ambulance - Result - Won 1-0.	
	7th		Coys devotes morning to cleaning up and kits inspecting. The Bngt which arrived on 6th were inspected by G.O.C 123rd Inf Bde. Afternoon - Coy Sports.	
	8th		Church Parade at 10am. A Rugby Match was held at 11.45am between H.Q. Coy & 'B' Coy - Result- H.Q. won 2 tries to nil. Afternoon was devoted to Games.	

Army Form C. 2118.

WAR DIARY
or
INTELLIGENCE SUMMARY.

(Erase heading not required.) REF MAP SHEET N° 5. JOURNAL

DECEMBER 1918

Place	Date	Hour	Summary of Events and Information	Remarks and references to Appendices
ST0007	9th		Battalion route march, strong bn parade, F.S.M.O. Roats - ST0007 - LESSINES - GRAMMONT - FRANKEN - SARLARDINGHE - REEKE - ST0007. Coys choose afternoon to sport. Special Orders issued regarding forthcoming march.	
	10R	Coys paraded under company arrangements BHQ & C Coy played the remainder of the Battalion at Rugby - result, BHQ + C, 4 pts; Remainder, 3 pts. Afternoon - Coy Sports. The following were awarded the French Croix de Guerre - Lieut. F. Hickman - Croix de Guerre à l'Ordre Division. 11315 A/CSM C Austin " " " 10993 CQMS CH Fielder " " " 40081 Sgt S Hanson " " Brigade 11905 CSM W Cuente " " Honours on Regiment.	
	11th	Coys paraded under Coy arrangements. Lieut. F. Hickman, CSM Austin, C.Q.M.S. Fielder were presented the French Croix De Guerre, by the Divisional Commander (Sir Sydney T.B. Lawford, K.C.B.) at 11:30 a.m. on the Station Square at Grammont. During the afternoon all troops were medically inspected by the medical Officer.	

ST0007

Army Form C. 2118.

WAR DIARY
or
INTELLIGENCE SUMMARY.
(Erase heading not required.)

DECEMBER. 1918.   Ref: Map Sheets 5+6 (TOURNAI + BRUSSELS.)

Place	Date	Hour	Summary of Events and Information	Remarks and references to Appendices
	12th		The march to Hannon started. Efroy was left at 09.45. Mons was reached at 13.00 when the battalion was billeted for the night. The weather was wet and the condition of the road, bad.	
	13.		March resumed at 09.15. Hondzocht was reached at 13.15; here billets were found for the night. The condition of weather and road considerably better.	
	14		March continued at 08.15. Genval WATERLOO was reached at 12.45. Weather and road conditions good. After tea the C.O. lectured half the battalion on the Battle of Waterloo.	
	15.		Church parade at 09.30. At 10.30 the C.O. lectured the rest of the battalion on the battle of Waterloo. Passes for the day to proceed to Brussels were granted to all men who wished to have same	

Army Form C. 2118.

WAR DIARY
or
INTELLIGENCE SUMMARY.
(Erase heading not required)

Title pages DECEMBER 1916   REF MAP - SHEET 6 (BRUSSELS)

Place	Date	Hour	Summary of Events and Information	Remarks and references to Appendices
	16		The march was continued at 08.00 hrs. The condition of the road was bad and the weather wet. The battlefield of WATERLOO was crossed before arriving at LOUPOIGNE at 13.30 where the battalion billeted for the night.	
	17		The march was resumed at 08.15 hrs. The battalion reached the resting area, SOMBREFFE, at 13.30 hrs. The road was good and the weather fine.	
	18		The battalion marched out of SOMBREFFE at 08.00 hrs. BOSSIÈRE was reached at 10.00 hrs. The road was good but it rained continuously during the march.	
	19		Bossière was left at 10.00 07.30 hrs LEUZE BRAINES was reached at 15.45 hrs. The weather was cold and wet — in places the road was bad. Dinner was eaten on the road.	
	20		The battalion marched from LEUZE at 07.30 hrs, reaching BRAINES at 14.30 hrs. Parts of the road were very bad; frequent	

Army Form C. 2118.

WAR DIARY
or
INTELLIGENCE SUMMARY.
(Erase heading not required.)

Title pages DECEMBER 1918.   REF MAP. SHEET 7 (LIEGE)

Place	Date	Hour	Summary of Events and Information	Remarks and references to Appendices
BRAIVES	21st		The morning was devoted to cleaning up, and afternoon to games.	
	22nd		Battalion attended Divine Service in the Cinema at 11am. Afternoon was devoted to Sports.	
	23rd		Battalion was bathed in LATINNE. Afternoon devoted to cleaning up. The undermentioned Officer was awarded the DISTINGUISHED ORDER for gallantry and devotion to duty in action. Lieut (acting Capt) J.C. HEDLEY. M.C.	
	24th		Battalion Parade under Coy arrangements. Afternoon devoted to Sports.	
	25th		Christmas Day. Coy Parades at Bn H.Q. for Divine Service at 9.30am. Comdg Officer visited all Companies at Dinner at 1pm.	

WAR DIARY
or
INTELLIGENCE SUMMARY.

(Erase heading not required.)

Army Form C. 2118.

REF: MAP SHEET 4. (LIÈGE)

DECEMBER 1918.

Place	Date	Hour	Summary of Events and Information	Remarks and references to Appendices
BRAIVES.	26th		Cleaning up and sanitation held during the morning sunday Coy arrangements. Games were held during the afternoon.	
	27th		Do.	Do.
	28th		Do.	Do.
	29th		Battalion paraded for Divine Service at 11am in the Cinema afternoon was devoted to games.	
	30th		Battalion parade for Route March at 9am - Bros-Fontin Route taken BRAIVES - LATINNE. FALLAIS. - VILLE-EN-HESBAYE. road junction NORTH of the B in HESBAYE - BRAIVES. afternoon - Football. Regt Leagues - A v J. Result 4 v. D.O.	
	31st		Coy parades under Coy arrangements. "A" Coy inspected at work by the Divisional Cmdr at 10.45am. Battalion inspects by C.O. at 11.15am. The following N.C.O.'s & Men were awarded decorations for Gallantry and devotion to duty in action:- 68730 Cpl Panay Bar to M.M. M.M. 11006 C.S.M. Pato. 205939 Cpl Wells D.C.M. 207939 Cpl Buzzard.	

W.A. Blount
Major
Comdg 11th Bn "The Queens" Regt.

LONDON DIVISION
(LATE 41ST DIVISION)
123RD INFY BDE

11TH BN Q.R. WEST SURREYS
1919 JAN ~~MAR 1919-FEB 1920~~
1919 SEP

To 1 Rhine Bde
Rhine Garrison

11 R.W. Surrey Rgt
Army Form C. 2118.

WAR DIARY
or
INTELLIGENCE SUMMARY.

(Erase heading not required.) REF MAPS SHEETS 9(LIEGE) GERMANY 33.

Place	Date	Hour	Summary of Events and Information	Remarks and references to Appendices
	JANUARY 1919			
	8th		The Battalion moves to Cologne Area to relieve the 2nd Bn. Canadian Infy. and parades ready to move off at 6.30 a.m. Order of March Hd Qrs, A, B, Bn H.Q., C, D. Transport preceded the Battn. by 2 hours. Bn marched to AMIENNE STATION where it entrained, and journey commenced at 1.10 p.m. The route taken was via LIEGE, — AIX LA CHAPPELLE — COLOGNE to TROISDORF where it detrained.	
	9th		Train arrived at TROISDORF at 9.45 a.m. Battn. had Breakfasts and after detraining was completely marched off at 11.30 a.m. to LOHMAR where it billeted for the night.	
SEELSCHEID AFTER Jan 10	10th		Battn. paraded at 7 a.m. to move to SEELSCHEID area to relieve 22nd Bn. Can: Infy. An Advanced Party went forward in lorries to take over posts in the front outposts. On arrival at destination at 9.45 a.m and duly into complete at 11.45 a.m Coys were located as follows:— Right Front Coy — "B" Coy at OBR. WENNESCHEID, Right Support Coy — "C" Coy with HQ at OBR. HOVEN. Left Support Coy — "D" Coy at POHLHAUSEN, Left Front Coy — "A" Coy at SEELSCHEID. Battn HQ Qrs at POST SEELSCHEID	

Army Form C. 2118.

WAR DIARY
or
INTELLIGENCE SUMMARY.
(Erase heading not required.) REF MAP SHEET 2.L. GERMANY

JANUARY 1919

Instructions regarding War Diaries and Intelligence Summaries are contained in F. S. Regs., Part II. and the Staff Manual respectively. Title pages will be prepared in manuscript.

Place	Date	Hour	Summary of Events and Information	Remarks and references to Appendices
##	11th		Support Coys carried out an hours parade and cleaned up. Front Line Coys were inspected by Coys Officers.	
	12th		Support Coy attended Church parade in the morning. At 11a.m. DESCRIPTION OF AREA:- The Battalion area is described as follows:- The ground is broken and hilly, intersected by roads, which at this season are flooded. The high ground in most cases is covered by woods and these numerous hamlets and very small villages, which are connected by tracks and in some cases by 2nd class roads.	
	13th		Support Coy paraded for two hours in the morning. Sports in the afternoon.	
	14th to 18th		Same programme	
SETELSCHELD	19th		Sunday.	
	20th to 23rd		As for 14th to 18th.	

WAR DIARY
or
INTELLIGENCE SUMMARY.

Ref: Map Sheet 2.L. Germany.

January 1919

Place	Date	Hour	Summary of Events and Information	Remarks and references to Appendices
	24th		Support Coy carries out 2 hours Bomb. during the morning.	
	24th		Battalion was relieved by 10th R.W. Kent Regt. and marched to LOHMAR when it was billetted for the night. Relief and move was completed at 16.15 hours.	
	25th		Battalion parades & marches off at 0900 hrs for LIND and reaches there at 1230 hrs. Batn. was billetted in a Pot.W. Camp. "A" Coy furnishes guard on River Rhine at Lulsdorf, Laribel and Zündorf. Strength of each guard - 2 B.O.'s & 12 men.	
	26th		Church Parade at 10.00 hrs. 1 Officer & 40 O.R. sent for attachment to 190 Bde R.F.A. until 9.W. Jan 1919.	
	27th		"B" Coy left Battalion to take over Fort IX in Westhoven area	
	28th		Coys carries out 2 hours parade during the morning	

Army Form C. 2118.

WAR DIARY
or
INTELLIGENCE SUMMARY.
(Erase heading not required.)

January 1919.

Place	Date	Hour	Summary of Events and Information	Remarks and references to Appendices
	29th		Coys carried out 2 hours training during the morning.	
	30th		Coys carried out 2 hours training. "D" Coy won the Shew in Drill Competition.	
	31st		Battalion left LIND Area at 0900 hours and marched to KALK-COLOGNE where it arrived at 1230 hrs. Battalion in billets in two Schools.	

C.A.Blount
Major
Comdg. 11th Bn. "The Queens" Regt.

Army Form C. 2118.

WAR DIARY
or
INTELLIGENCE SUMMARY.

(Erase heading not required.)

11th The Queens

Ref: Map Sheet Cyprus Z.L. 1/100,000

WDL 34

FEBRUARY 1919.

Place	Date	Hour	Summary of Events and Information	Remarks and references to Appendices
COLN - KALK	1st	—	Battalion spent day in cleaning up and kitting Inspection. Fourteen Other Ranks proceed on Demobilization.	
	2nd	—	Church Service was held in Billets at 9.30am. Eleven O.Rks proceed on Demobilization.	
	3rd	—	Battalion Practised Ceremonial Drill for Foundation of Colours. Afternoon — Divisional Inter Coy Competition. Result "D" Coy 3rd. Major R.G. Thompson, Six O.Rks proceed on Demobilization. "A" Coy relieved "B" Coy at FORT IX.	
	4th	—	Battalion Practised Ceremonial Drill which was attended by the G.O.C. 123rd Inf. Bde. Six O.Rks proceed on Demobilization.	
	5th	—	Battalion Practised Ceremonial Drill which was attended by the Divisional Commdt.	
	6th	—	Battalion Practised Ceremonial Drill on the Exerzier Platz and were attended by the Divisional Commdr.	

Army Form C. 2118.

WAR DIARY
or
INTELLIGENCE SUMMARY.
(Erase heading not required.)

Instructions regarding War Diaries and Intelligence Summaries are contained in F.S. Regs., Part II. and the Staff Manual respectively. Title pages will be prepared in manuscript.

FEBRUARY 1919. Ref. Map Sheet – GERMANY 2.L.

Place	Date	Hour	Summary of Events and Information	Remarks and references to Appendices
COLN – KALK.	7th		Day was devoted to cleaning up equipment, clothing etc. Ten other Ranks proceeded on Demobilization.	
	8th		Battalion inspected by County Officer afterwards Lecture was given by Lieut. T.P. YOUNG on "France" and the Speech "People" was given in the Hall at 241 KALKER HAUPT STRASSE. 8 O.Rs proceeded on Demobilization.	
	9th		Divine Service held at 11.30 in the Victoria Cinema, KALKER HAUPT STRASSE. 11 O.Rs proceeded on Demobilization.	
	10th		Battalion paraded for Armoured Parade, at which the P.O.C. 120th Sub/Div. was present. Lieut A.W. HOOLEY reported for duty, previously serving to before the Battalion.	
	11th		The Battalion paraded on the EXERSIER PLATZ, when it was presented the Colour by the Army Cmdr., Genl. Sir H. PLUMER. G.C.B. who gave a speech on the occasion of The Queen. The Colour Party was Lieut G.N. BRADNOCK. Escort – C.S.M. GARRATT. – C.S.M. AUSTIN	

Army Form C. 2118.

WAR DIARY
or
INTELLIGENCE SUMMARY.
(Erase heading not required.)

Ref. Prep. Sheet. Germany 2.L

February 1919

Place	Date	Hour	Summary of Events and Information	Remarks and references to Appendices
COLN - KALK	12th		The Brigade Comd. Br. Genl. M. KEMP NEROH DSO. MC, presented the Belgian Croix de Guerre to a number of Officers & NCO's of the Bn. at 10.30 a.m., 2nd Lieut. BROMHEAD and Cpl. GEARY were amongst the recipients.	
	13th		Battalion devotes day to improving equipment, etc; also settles 14 O.R.'s proceeds on Demobilization.	
	14th		Education Classes held under Education Officer (Lt. MAK). 10 O.R.'s proceeded on Demobilization. Information received from 36th C.C.S. to the effect that Major J. WINDHAM WRIGHT died at 7.45 a.m. Cause - Pneumonia.	
	15th		Day devoted to Interior Economy & Kit Inspection. 7 O.R.'s proceeded on Demobilization.	
	16th		Divine Service was held in the VIKTORIA CINEMA at 10 a.m. 14 O.R.'s proceeded on Demobilization	

Army Form C. 2118.

WAR DIARY
or
INTELLIGENCE SUMMARY.
(Erase heading not required.)

Ref Map Sheet Germany L.2.

February 1919

Place	Date	Hour	Summary of Events and Information	Remarks and references to Appendices
	17th		Battalion carried out ordinary routine, Education Classes, Games etc in the afternoon. 15.0 T.M. demobilized.	
	18th		During the morning Battalion carried out ordinary routine. In the afternoon the funeral of the late MAJOR J. WINDHAM-WRIGHT took place, and who was buried with full military honours.	
	19th		Coys at the disposal of Coy Comdrs. Games in the afternoon.	
	20th		Battalion carried out ordinary routine, musketry etc. Afternoon – Games.	
	21st		Ordinary routine, and musketry on the Range at BRUCK Afternoon – Games	
	22nd		Cleaning up, Inspections, etc carried out. Afternoon – Games.	

Army Form C. 2118.

WAR DIARY
or
INTELLIGENCE SUMMARY.
(Erase heading not required.)

Ref. Map Sheet *Germany 2L*

February 1919

Instructions regarding War Diaries and Intelligence Summaries are contained in F. S. Regs., Part II. and the Staff Manual respectively. Title pages will be prepared in manuscript.

Place	Date	Hour	Summary of Events and Information	Remarks and references to Appendices
	23rd		Divine Service held in VIKTORIA CINEMA, KALKER HAURTE STRASSE at 10.30 a.m.	
	24th		Battalion carries out ordinary routine & bathed at KAISER WILHIEM Baths at DEUTZ. Afternoon – Games	
	25th		Battalion relieves 10th R.W. Kent Regt as Battalion on duty and took over all Guards, Piquets etc in and around KALK.	
	26th		} Battalion on Duty.	
	27th			
	28th			

J.A. Newworth?
Major
Commdg 11th Bn The Queens Regt

Army Form C. 2118.

WAR DIARY
or
INTELLIGENCE SUMMARY.

(Erase heading not required.) Ref: Maps Sheet. Germany 2L 1/100 000

March 1919

Place: COLN - KALK

Date	Hour	Summary of Events and Information	Remarks and references to Appendices
1st		Battalion on Duty.	
2nd		Ditto.	
3rd		Ditto.	
4th		Battalion relieved of Guards by 23rd Middlesex Regt.	
5th		Battalion carried out ordinary parades and cleaning up. The following were awarded the Military Medal for gallantry:- 11019 Cpl S. Wallace, 10892 Cpl C. Wheeler, 40059 L.C. Stanford, C. 25634 Pte J. Carter.	
6th		Battalion carried out Musketry on the Range at BRUCK. The following joined the Battn from 6th Bn:- Lieut- N.J. BARRE Lieut T.C. CROWE, and 23 ORs.	
7th		Battalion carries out ordinary training	

Army Form C. 2118.

WAR DIARY
or
INTELLIGENCE SUMMARY.
(Erase heading not required.)

Ref Map Sheet Germany 2.L. 1/100 000

Instructions regarding War Diaries and Intelligence Summaries are contained in F. S. Regs., Part II. and the Staff Manual respectively. Title pages will be prepared in manuscript.

March 1919

Place	Date	Hour	Summary of Events and Information	Remarks and references to Appendices
COLN – KALK.	8th		Battalion carried out Inspection and Interior Economy.	
	9th		Battalion attended Divn Series in the Victoria Cinema KALKER HAUPTE STR. at 1000 hrs.	
	10th		Battalion carried out ordinary parades. A Section Competition was carried out in the afternoon on BRUCK Range, which was won by "D" Coy.	
	11th		Battalion carried out ordinary training. Training Captain 5.3.19. (Authy B.O. LIEUT. & QR MR: B.W. JORDAN M.C. Promotis Captain 12/203/5 dt 6.3.19.	
	12th		Battalion carried out musketry at Bruck Range in the morning. In afternoon a great number of the Battalion went to BONN to witness a Corps Boxing Competition. The following Officers the Battalion from the 6th Bn. Capt. H.D. GARDINER. & 7 Other Ranks.	

Army Form C. 2118.

WAR DIARY
or
INTELLIGENCE SUMMARY
(Erase heading not required.)

March 1919. Ref. Maps Sheet Germany 2.L. 100,000

Place	Date	Hour	Summary of Events and Information	Remarks and references to Appendices
	13th		Battalion carries out ordinary training, and ⅔ outposts in F.S.M.O. by the County Officer.	
	14th		Battalion was inspected by the Brigade Comdr at 11.45 hrs on the EXERZIER PLATZ, HOHENBURG.	
	15th		Battalion over all guard and escort duties of Bn. on Duty. The following formed the Battalion from the 6th Battn:- Lieut. E.F. REEVES M.C. Lieut W.H. WILLIAMS, + 49 O.Rks. The following officers were accepted for the Army of Occupation :- Lieuts: (a/Capts) H.C. WILLIAMS, C.J.M. PAIGE D.S.O M.C. C.H. BROADHEAD, LIEUTS. L.G. MAUDLING MC, W.C. LESTER SMITH, D.C. McBRIDE, D.W. COLLYER, E.C. WILLIAMS DCM, S.V.J. COULSON, W MAY. W.E. HUNTER. D. JACKSON MC, A. TURKINGTON MM. C.A. CLARK, V. WEAVING G. TOBBS. 12 O.Rs. proceeds on demobilization	

Army Form C. 2118.

WAR DIARY
or
INTELLIGENCE SUMMARY.

(Erase heading not required.) *Rgt Maj. Shed. Germany Z.L. 100 or so*

March 1919

Place	Date	Hour	Summary of Events and Information	Remarks and references to Appendices
	16th		Battalion on duty. 11 ORs proceeds on Demobilization and 6 ORs on re-enlistment leave. Lieut H.G. PENFOLD joined 1st Battn from 6th Bn.	
	17th		Battalion on duty.	
	18th		Ditto.	
	19th		Ditto.	
	20th		Ditto.	
	21st		Ditto.	
	22nd		Ditto. 4 ORs proceeds on Demobilization and 5 ORs on re-enlistment leave.	
	23rd		Battalion relieved off duty by 23rd Bn. Middlesex Rgt.	
	24th		Battalion relieved 23rd Middlesex of all guards.	

Army Form C. 2118.

WAR DIARY
or
INTELLIGENCE SUMMARY.
(Erase heading not required.)

Ref. Map Sheet January 2L 100,000

March 1919.

Instructions regarding War Diaries and Intelligence Summaries are contained in F. S. Regs., Part II and the Staff Manual respectively. Title pages will be prepared in manuscript.

Place	Date	Hour	Summary of Events and Information	Remarks and references to Appendices
	25th		Battalion on duty. Orders received for move to LINDLAR on 28th. Lieut B WOMACK M.C. joined from 6th Bn.	
	26th		Battalion relieved of guards by 17th Bn. R. Fusiliers.	
	27th		Battalion spent day in cleaning up & preparing for the move.	
	28th		Battalion paraded at 08.20 hrs and march to COIN-KALK Station where it entrained at 08.30. Leaving at 09.10 hrs arrived at LINDLAR at 12.35 p.m. and relieves the 23rd R. Fusiliers at in the Left Sub Sector. Coys were disposed as follows:- 'A' Coy - Right front, supported by 'B' Coy. 'D' Coy - Left front, supported by 'C' Coy. Bn Hd Qrs - LINDLAR. 18 O.Rs transferred on Demobilization to 6 O.R. on re enlistment clause.	

Army Form C. 2118.

WAR DIARY
or
INTELLIGENCE SUMMARY

(Erase heading not required.)

Army Form C. 2118.

Place	Date	Hour	Summary of Events and Information	Remarks and references to Appendices
March 1919	29th		No alteration.	
	30th		Divine Service held in LINDLAR School at 10.00hrs to all available men.	
	31st		The Commanding Officer inspected posts.	

April 1st 1919

W.N. Blount
Lieut Colonel
Comdg 11th Duke of Edinburgh's

WAR DIARY
or
INTELLIGENCE SUMMARY

Army Form C. 2118.

April 1919   Ref: Map Sheet, Germany 2.L.

Place	Date	Hour	Summary of Events and Information	Remarks and references to Appendices
	1st		The 52nd Bn The Queen's Regt joined the Battalion as reinforcements, and were absorbed. The 52nd Bn was composed of 39 Officers and 903 ORs, and were posted as follows:- A to A, B to B, C to C, & D to D. They were commanded by Lieut Colonel J.W. Jeffreys D.S.O. Durham Light Infantry.	
	2nd		The outpost line was taken by the Divisional Commander (Sir S.T.B. Lawford. K.C.B) and certain posts inspected. Lieut Colonel J.W. Jeffreys D.S.O. assumed command of the Battn.	
	3rd		The Battalion carried out training etc, and B & C Coys Parades working parties on the Groin line of resistance. Recreational Games in the afternoon.	
	4th		As for the 3rd	

Army Form C. 2118.

WAR DIARY
or
INTELLIGENCE SUMMARY

(Erase heading not required.)

Army April 1919 Key Map - Sheet Germany 24

Place	Date	Hour	Summary of Events and Information	Remarks and references to Appendices
LINDLAR	5th		Battalion Games and training etc. also working parties. Lieut Colonel R.T. LEE, C.M.G. D.S.O. having joined the Battalion assumed command from this day.	
	6th		"Band 'C' Coys attended Church Parade at 10.30 hrs in the courtyard of Bn. H.Q. Mess. Afternoon was devoted to Games	
	7th		Training was carried out, also work on Main Line of Resistance. Games in the afternoon.	
	8th		Do	
	9th		Training & Education was carried out. 'B' Coy bathed at ENGELSKIRCHEN. Transport was inspected by the Brigade Commander.	
	10th		Training etc was carried out, also work on main line of Resistance. The Transport was inspected by the Divisional Commander at 14.30 hrs.	

Army Form C. 2118.

WAR DIARY
or
INTELLIGENCE SUMMARY.
(Erase heading not required.)

Ref Map Sheet – Germany 2c.

April 1919

Place	Date	Hour	Summary of Events and Information	Remarks and references to Appendices
	11th		Training, education etc carried out. Inter Coy reliefs were carried out as follows:- "B" relieves "A" "C" relieves "D".	Green Envs.
	12th		Day was devoted to cleaning up, inspections etc. Recreational Training during afternoon	
	13th		No Church Parade was held owing to inclement weather.	
	14th		The Outpost Line was visited by the new Brigade Guard. (Br Genl DUDGEON) commencing at 14.00 hrs. Inter Platoon Football Competition during the afternoon	
	15th		Training, Education & work was carried out. Inter Platoon Football Competition commenced during the afternoon	

Army Form C. 2118.

WAR DIARY
or
INTELLIGENCE SUMMARY.

(Erase heading not required.)

Ref Map Sheet Germany 2L

April 1919

Place	Date	Hour	Summary of Events and Information	Remarks and references to Appendices
LINDLAR	16th		Training, education & work 1700 carried out - inter-platoon football competition in afternoon. A Coy bathed at ENGELSKIRCHEN.	
	17th		Training, education & work carried out - inter-platoon competition in football. Middle afternoon. HQ Coy & Bn/HQ staff bathed at ENGELSKIRCHEN. Pay/parade.	
	18th (Good Friday)		Observed as Sunday. Divine Service was held.	
	19th		Training, education & work was carried out. Football in afternoon - inter-Company match.	
	20th		No church parade was held owing to bad weather.	
	21st		As on 19th. Col. T.H. Jeffrys proceeded to 9 C'bn D.L.I. Major Sir H.R. Blount proceeded to England for demobilization.	
	22nd		As on 21st.	
	23rd		As on 22nd. A Coy & half HQ Coy bathed at ENGELSKIRCHEN	
	24th		Training, education, work carried out & recreational training in afternoon. D Coy & remainder of HQ Coy bathed at ENGELSKIRCHEN.	

WAR DIARY or INTELLIGENCE SUMMARY

(Erase heading not required.)

Army Form C. 2118.

Ref Maps Sheet — Germany 2 L

April 1919

Place	Date	Hour	Summary of Events and Information	Remarks and references to Appendices
	25th		A party of 2 Band & party of 60 all ranks proceeded to COLOGNE for Rhine trips. Pay Parade.	
	26th		As for 25th. Committee formed to carry out duties of P.R.I. Sports. Band & amusements & Officers leave fund. Party from Rhine trip returned at night. Battalion orient.	
	27th		Church parade held in orient hall owing to bad weather. Sports meeting held.	
	28th		Training, education & P.T. carried out & recreational training afternoon. 200 ors proceeded to COLN-KALK to Dirt Race Meeting — returned at night.	
	29th		As for 28th.	
	30th		Relieved by 10th Bn The Queens On completion of relief this battalion 2/4th Queens on Right Sub-Sect. Headquarters ENGELSKIRCHEN. Relief completed by 19.30 hrs.	See Signal Orders

R. T. Roe
Lieut Colonel
Comdg 2/4th Bn The Queens (R.W.S.) Regt.

WAR DIARY
INTELLIGENCE SUMMARY

Army Form C. 2118.

Ref Map Germany 35 SE/NE

Queen

May 1919

ENGELSKIRCHEN AREA

Place	Date	Hour	Summary of Events and Information	Remarks and references to Appendices
	1st		B'd Coys. bathed & spent remainder of day clearing up. Recreational training in afternoon. A cinema was given in the evening which men attended. Reports all alright, was given in by the sentry of a Right Guard Coy post.	
	2nd		Training & education carried out — Inter. exercises to 2 Plats of B.Coy. Boxed and they provided recreational training in afternoon. A lecture on venereal disease was given in the afternoon. Pay parade. 9 ORs proceeded to England to demobilization.	
	3rd		Training & education carried out – 2 Plats of B.Coy. find men carried out Recreational training in afternoon. 3 other ranks joined from 8th Bn the Queen's. Aeroplane and Brigade Ammunition fatigue party supplied to assist at Brigade School. Fatigue party supplied to bivouac.	
	4th		Church parade. Service held in Lutheran Church at Bergische Schule.	
	5th		Training & education carried out. Recreational training in afternoon. Lewis Station platoon competition held in morning — won by platoon of C Coy. The winner Coln No.16 platoon — men entered in task by 3 points.	
	15		Training & education carried out — ceremonial parade — Recreational training in afternoon. 8 ORs joined from 8th Bn The Queens. 2 officers and 10 2/Lt's London Regt.	

Capt A.C. Williams Sh.H. Dale
Major Arty Colyer 2 Lt H.R. Atkinson
" A.J. Blair
" P.D. Baynes

8th London Regt.
Lieut. Bascombe
C.W. Haraford
2/Lt M.S. Kelley
L.A. Chanden

WAR DIARY
or
INTELLIGENCE SUMMARY

Army Form C. 2118.

Ry Traps Germany B₃ S+N.K.

May 1919

Place	Date	Hour	Summary of Events and Information	Remarks and references to Appendices
	4/5		Training & education carried out. Received training in afternoon. Working parties supplied for baths & Brigade School. No bathing carried out owing to baths being out of order. Mounted Inspection carried out.	
	8/5		Training & education carried out – 2 Coys fired on range at EHRESHOVEN. Received training in afternoon. Working parties supplied for baths & Brigade School. Bathing in afternoon. 30 ORs arrived from 8th Bn The Queens Regt. & 150 ORs proceeded to 7/7 M.B. 2 Rondon Brigade.	
	9/5		Training & Education carries out. Working parties furnished for R.E. and Bus Schools Thereafter during the afternoon.	
	10/5		Ditto.	
	11/5		Divine Service was held as follows:— Roman Catholic at Castle Church at 09.30. Church of England, in Obstacle Course field at 09.30. Presbyterian & Free Church in Lutheran Church at 11.30.	

ENGELSKIRCHEN

Army Form C. 2118.

WAR DIARY
or
INTELLIGENCE SUMMARY.
(Erase heading not required.)

Ref. Map:- Germany 93, S.E. & N.E.

May 1919.

Place	Date	Hour	Summary of Events and Information	Remarks and references to Appendices
Engelskirchen	12th		Training and Education carried out. Recreation during the afternoon. Working Parties as before.	
	13th		Training & Education carried out. 'B' & 'C' Coys carried out an Advanced Guard Scheme in the morning. Afternoon was devoted to Recreation & Education.	
	14th		'B' Coy relieves 'A' Coy and 'C' Coy relieves 'D' in the outpost line. Half Battalion at Baths. Afternoon - Recreation.	
	15th		Training and Education carried out. Recreation Leicester in the afternoon. Half Batt. Bathing. A & D Coys fired on the Range at EHRESHOVEN.	
	16th		Training & Education carried out. Recreation & Education in the afternoon.	

Army Form C. 2118.

WAR DIARY
or
INTELLIGENCE SUMMARY.
(Erase heading not required.)

Ref. Map. Germany 5s. SE, NE

May 1919

Place	Date	Hour	Summary of Events and Information	Remarks and references to Appendices
Enge/Iskirgen	17th		Training and Education carried out. Recreation in the afternoon. A & D Coys were inspected on parade by the Corps Commander at 11.15 hrs.	
	18th		Divine Service was held as follows:- Roman Catholics in Catholic Church at 09.30. Church of England, in Obstacle Course Field at 09.30 hours. Presbyterians & Free Church in Lutheran Church at 11.30 hrs	
	19th		Training and Education carried out. Working Parties as before. Recreation & Education in the afternoon.	
	20th		"A" & "B" Coy carried out an Advanced Guard Scheme. Remainder at Training & Education. Recreation & Education carried out during the afternoon.	

Army Form C. 2118.

WAR DIARY
or
INTELLIGENCE SUMMARY
(Erase heading not required.)

Ref: Map Sheet Germany 3s 55 Y NE

May 1919

Place	Date	Hour	Summary of Events and Information	Remarks and references to Appendices
Engelskirchen	21st		"B" Coy carries out an Advanced Guard Scheme. Remainder at Training & Education. Half Batts at Baths. Recreation during Afternoon.	
	22nd		"A" & "D" Coys carries out musketry on EHRESHOVEN Range. Remainder did Training & Education. Half Batts Baths. Recreation & Education during the afternoon.	
	23rd		Training and Education carried out in the morning. Afternoon Recreation.	
	24th		Ditto. Ditto.	
	25th		Divine Service as for last Sunday.	

Army Form C. 2118.

WAR DIARY
or
INTELLIGENCE SUMMARY.

(Erase heading not required.) Ref Map Germany 3s N.E & S.E.

May 1919.

Place	Date	Hour	Summary of Events and Information	Remarks and references to Appendices
ENGELSKIRCHEN	26th		Training & Education carried out. Recreation & Education in the afternoon.	
	27th		A Short Route March was carried out by A.H. & H.Q. parading at 05.00 hrs. returning at 11.00 hrs. Recreation & Education carried out during afternoon.	
	28th		The late Battalion Relief were carried out as follows:- 2/4 "B" Queens relieved 10th Bn. Queens, 11th Bn. "The Queens" relieved 10th Bn "The Queens" relieved 2/4 "B" Bn. The Queens. The Battn on completion of relief moved into Reserve at EMBESHOVEN, and occupied Billets vacated by the 2/4 "B" Bn. Lt Colonel R.T. Lee, D.M.G. D.S.O. was admitted to Hospl.	
EMBESHOVEN	29th		Battalion carried out Training and also Bathes at ENGELSKIRCHEN. Recreation & Education in the afternoon.	

Army Form C. 2118.

WAR DIARY
or
INTELLIGENCE SUMMARY.
(Erase heading not required.)

Place: Rly Head - Germany 35. NE & SE.
May 1919

Place	Date	Hour	Summary of Events and Information	Remarks and references to Appendices
	30th		Training & Education was carried out, and Recreation & Education in the afternoon. Firing on the long range was carried out by "B" & "C" Coys.	
	31st		Battalion moves and repitches the Camp, in the area S. 17. 37.	

R.P. Newman
Captain
O/c & 11th Bn "The Queens Rgt"

Army Form C. 2118.

WAR DIARY
or
INTELLIGENCE SUMMARY.

(Erase heading not required.) Ref: Map Shut. SE & NE. 53. Germany

JUNE 1919

Place	Date	Hour	Summary of Events and Information	Remarks and references to Appendices
LARKSHOVEN	1st		Church Parade held in Camp at 11.45 hours.	
	2nd		Training and Education was carried out during the morning. Recreation in the Afternoon.	
	3rd		The Birthday of H.M. The King was celebrated by a Special Ceremonial Parade at 09.00 hours. The Battalion was inspected by the Comdg Officer, and the Royal Salute & three cheers were given for His Majesty. The rest of the day was treated as a holiday and Battalion Sports were held.	
	4th		Training and Education was carried out during the morning. Recreation in the Afternoon. Hockey Parties were also furnished for R.E.'s	
	5th		Training & Education. Colonel R.T. Lee CMG DSO proceeded to England and struck off the Strength.	

Army Form C. 2118.

WAR DIARY
or
INTELLIGENCE SUMMARY.

(Erase heading not required.) Ref. Map Sheet. S3. S.E. & N.E. (Germany)

June 1919.

Place	Date	Hour	Summary of Events and Information	Remarks and references to Appendices
	7th		Training and Education took place in the morning, and Recreation in the afternoon.	
	8th		Church Parade took place in Camp at 11.30 hrs.	
	9th		Training and Education in the morning, also working parties furnished for R.E. Recreation during the afternoon.	
EHRESHOVEN	10th		The Battalion paraded at 08.00 hrs for Route march. Route was UNTER VILKERATH. - BOCHMÜHLE. - MTE BACH. - EHRESHOVEN. Working parties furnished for R.E. Recreation cleared the afternoon.	
	11th		Training & Education during the morning, also bathing at ENGELSKIRCHEN. Recreation during the afternoon.	
	12th		Training & Education during the morning, also bathing. Recreation during the afternoon.	

Army Form C. 2118.

WAR DIARY
or
INTELLIGENCE SUMMARY.
(Erase heading not required.)

Ref. Map Sheet S.3. S.E.T.N.E

Instructions regarding War Diaries and Intelligence Summaries are contained in F. S. Regs., Part II. and the Staff Manual respectively. Title pages will be prepared in manuscript.

Place	Date	Hour	Summary of Events and Information	Remarks and references to Appendices
EHRESHOVEN	13th		Training & Education took place during the morning. Recreation during the afternoon.	
	14th		A Battalion Ceremonial Parade was held in the morning. Recreation during the afternoon.	
	15th		Church Parade was held in Camp at 11.45 hrs.	
	16th		Lt Colonel F.C. LONSBOURNE C.M.G. D.S.O. arrived and assumed Command of the Battalion. The Battalion paraded in Fighting Order at 10.30 hrs and was inspected by the G.O.C. in C. (Gen. Sir William ROBERTSON G.C.B.) and afterwards marched past in fours. Recreation during the afternoon.	
	17th		"A" & "B" Coys. commenced the General Musketry Course, remainder carried out training and education, and recreation during the afternoon.	

June 1919

Army Form C. 2118.

WAR DIARY
or
INTELLIGENCE SUMMARY.
(Erase heading not required.)

June 1919. Ref. Map Sheet S.3. SEINE (Germany)

Place	Date	Hour	Summary of Events and Information	Remarks and references to Appendices
EHRESHOVEN.	18th		Orders having been received that the Battalion will move forward on "T" Day i.e. 20th July 1919, all surplus stores etc collected. S.A.A. made up to 120 rds per man and iron rations issued.	See O.O. Rc attached.
	19th		Inspection being suspended, training is being carried on. Message received that "T" Day has been postponed till Monday 23rd	
	20th		Training & Education resumed. The following message was received from G.O.C in C. "The Commander in Chief has expressed his satisfaction at the Inspection held by him on 16th inst, and wishes at the Inspection and turn out of the Battalion the fact to be conveyed to the Officers, N.C.O. and men concerned.	
	21st		Training & Education carried out during the morning & recreation during the afternoon.	

Army Form C. 2118.

WAR DIARY
or
INTELLIGENCE SUMMARY.
(Erase heading not required.)

Ref Map Sheet S.3. SE & NE. (Germany)

June 1919

Place	Date	Hour	Summary of Events and Information	Remarks and references to Appendices
	22nd		Church Parade held in the Gardens of the "Schloss" at 12.15 hrs.	
	23rd		"T" Bay again postponed. Training etc. carried out. Recreation in the afternoon.	
	24th		Training etc carried out in the morning. Recreation in the afternoon	
EHRESHOVEN	25th		Do Do Do	
	26th		Do Do Do	
	27th		"A" & "B" Coys honoured the General Remembrance. Carried out training & education. Recreation during the afternoon.	

Army Form C. 2118.

WAR DIARY
or
INTELLIGENCE SUMMARY.

(Erase heading not required.) Ref: Map Sheet. 53 SE & NE (Germany)

Place	Date	Hour	Summary of Events and Information	Remarks and references to Appendices
EHRESHOVEN	28th	—	'A' & 'B' Coys at musketry remainder at Training etc. Revielle during afternoon. Wire received at 20.40 hrs notifying that Peace had been signed.	
	29th		Church Service was held in the Dining Huts of C & D Coys. 'B' Coy at musketry.	
	30th		'A' & 'B' Coys at musketry, remainder at Training etc. Recreation during the afternoon.	

R.J. Newman Capt?
Lt Colonel
Comdg 11th Bn The Queens Regt

S E C R E T.

11TH BATTALION "THE QUEEN'S" (R.W.S) REGIMENT
==

INSTRUCTIONS TO ACCOMPANY OPERATION ORDER No. 7.
(Dated 17th June 1919)

19th June 1919.
————————————

1. Copies of "Instructions to Troops", British Army of the Rhine, have been issued to Companies at the rate of one copy per Officer. The instructions relating to the action of N.C.Os and men contained therein will be <u>thoroughly</u> explained to all ranks.
 ACKNOWLEDGE.

==

[signature]

Captain.
Adjutant 11th Bn "The "ueen's" (R.W.S) Regiment.

S E C R E T.

11TH BATTALION "THE QUEEN'S" (R.W.S.) REGIMENT.

INSTRUCTIONS TO ACCOMPANY OPERATION ORDER No. 7.
(Dated 17th June 1919).

22nd June 1919.

1. On "J" plus 1 day, Officer Commanding "D" Company will detail 2 Bus loads, i.e. 6 Sections, to relieve 6 Sections of "D" Company, 10th Bn. Queen's Regt. at SUNDERN. One Section will man the Post Office Exchange at SUNDERN.
The Busses of this party will remain with them until they are relieved, and then convey them to the Battalion.

2. A table showing the dispositions of Companies in the Bus Column is issued herewith.

Captain.
Adjutant 11th Battalion "The Queen's" (R.W.S) Regiment.

Copies issued to all
recipients of Operation Orders.

SECRET.   Copy No. 16

OPERATION ORDER No.7.

11th Battalion "THE QUEEN'S" (Royal West Surrey) Regiment.
                                                    17th June 1919.

Ref. Map.Sheet No.59. 1/200,000.

INTENTION.   In the event of a general advance the 2nd London Brigade
             Group will be the leading Brigade of the London Division.
             The object of the advance will be to secure complete control
             of German Railway Systems up to the valley of the RUHR that are
             considered essential for a further advance.

INFORMATION. The 2nd London Brigade will commence the advance on Friday
             20th instant (J.Day).
             The Advance Guard will be furnished by 10th Bn "The Queen's"
             (R.W.S) Regt., together with Artillery and Cavalry under Command
             of Colonel R.O'H.Livesay, C.M.G., D.S.O,

---

1.   In accordance with the above the Battalion will move forward on
     "J" day, which is Friday, the 20th instant.

2.   The Battalion, (less "B" and "C" Companies) will form part of the
     Main Body and will follow the 2nd London L.T.M.B. in the Column.
     "B" Company will rejoin the Battalion as soon as relieved by the
     Cavalry on the 20th instant.

3.   The following will not accompany the Battalion, but will remain as
     Details at ENGELSKIRCHEN until further orders:-
     Lieut.B.A.Shortman. Commanding Details.
     Lieut.W.May. Band & Drums. The Range Wardens will remain behind
     and live   with the Camp Guard.
     These Details will be left with 2 days' rations, and Iron Ration.

4.   The Battalion will march to ENGELSKIRCHEN and embus. There are
     32 busses and 3 spare, for the conveyance of the Battalion.
     The spare busses will move empty and not be used, and will be
     distributed along the Column at the rate of 1 in 10.
     The Billetting Party under the Command of 2/Lieut.F.W.J.Heave,MC.
     will proceed in advance of the Battalion and allot busses to
     Companies etc.

5.   On Thursday the 19th instant, "A" Company will proceed to
     ENGELSKIRCHEN and relieve the administrative posts now held by
     10th Bn"The Queen's" (R.W.S) Regt.
     Further details will be issued to this Company.

6.   All busses will be clearly marked with"Company"also"Headquarters".

7.   "B" Company is detailed as escort to R.F.A., Officer Commanding
     "B" Company will report to O.C. 187th Brigade, R.F.A. for
     instructions on Thursday, 19th instant, at ENGELSKIRCHEN.

8.   Officer Commanding "C" Company will detail 2 platoons as escort
     to No.3 Coy. Divisional Train. Officer Commanding "C" Company
     will report to O.C. No.3 Company Divisional Train for instructions
     on Thursday, the 19th instant, at ENGELSKIRCHEN.

9.   Two platoons of "C" Company under the Command of Captain J.C.
     Hedley, DSO.,MC., will be Rear Guard to the Brigade.

10. All Lewis Guns will be taken on the Busses.

11. On Friday, 20th instant, the Brigade will move to ATTENDORN via
     OLPE.
     On "J" plus 1 day it will move to ARNSBERG.

Page 2.

OPERATION ORDER No.7. (Continued)

12. During the advance Aeroplanes of No.12 Squadron R.A.F. will reconnoitre the ground to the front.
 If an aeroplane wishes to locate <u>our Infantry</u>, it will fly low, at the same time sounding a Klaxon Horn (a series of "A's"). Troops will respond by flashing <u>tin discs</u> which will be issued. Contact planes will carry a black streamer at the bottom of the left hand plane.
 During the advance Red Verey Lights (1"). will be used by troops to signal that their advance is being resisted by the enemy.

13. Full use will be made of Visual Signalling as laying of cables during a rapid advance is wasteful and unnecessary.

14. Officers Commanding Companies etc. on arrival at destination each day, will inform all ranks the position of their Company and Battalion Headquarters.

15. During the advance a halt will be made for 10 minutes at every clock hour, and during those halts the leading Company will be responsible for the protection of the right flank, and the rear Company will be responsible for the left flank. One Platoon will be used for this protection, and will wear their equipment doing so.
 Officers Commanding Companies on escort duty will be responsible for similar protection.

16. A billeting party of 1 N.C.O. per Company and Battalion Headquarters under 2/Lieut.E.W.J.Neave, M.C., will travel with Battalion Hdqrs, and will report to the Staff Captain at the Burgomaster's Office at ATTENDORN on Friday, 20th inst., immediately after arrival.

17. It is stated that no serious opposition is likely, and it is not considered that there are any organised enemy troops in the area to be traversed. Nevertheless, as far as it is consistant with a rapid advance, all possible military precautions will be taken. Troops encountered will be disarmed, and any attempted resistance will at once be vigorously overcome.
 The Officer Commanding every party of our troops is held responsible that due precaution is taken to <u>guard against surprise</u> by day and by night. Detachments will be sufficiently strong to provide the necessary guards and sentrys.

18. The 1st Line Transport, Brigaded under the Command of 2/Lieut.A.H. Fitzgerald, will follow the Brigade Supply Lorry Column.

19. Situation reports will be forwarded to the Adjutant by 0400 hours and 1400 hours daily. The report at 1400 hours will include capture of prisoners and other material for previous 24 hours.

20. Officers Commanding Companies will render a return to the Adjutant by 1600 hours Wednesday, 18th inst., showing:-
 1. Numbers of all ranks to be embussed.
 2. Strength and location of guards left behind, in detail.
 3. Strength of any other personnel left behind in ENGELSKIRCHEN.

****

(Sgd) T.P.NEWMAN. Captain.
Adjutant 11th Battalion "THE QUEEN'S" (R.W.S) Regiment.

DISTRIBUTION.
1. Commdg.Officer.
2. Second in C.
3. Adjutant.
4. O.C. "A" Coy.
5. O.C. "B" Coy.
6. O.C. "C" Coy.
7. O.C. "D" Coy.
8. O.C. "H.Qrs" Coy.
9. Signal Officer.
10. 2/Lt.E.W.J.Neave.MC.
11. Lieut.B.A.Shortman.
12. 2nd Lon.Inf.Bde.
13. 10th Bn Queen's R.W.S.Regt.
14. R.S.M.
15. File.
16. War Diary.

ADMINISTRATIVE INSTRUCTIONS
by
Lieut.Colonel F.C.Longbourne. C.M.G. D.S.O. Comdg.11th Battalion.
"THE QUEEN'S" (Royal West Surrey) Regiment.

17th June 1919.

1. RATIONS. Fresh Rations will be drawn tomorrow for 19th instant.
Preserved Rations will be drawn on 19th for consumption on 21st.
The Hard Ration in hand will be consumed on the 20th inst.

2. AMMUNITION. All N.C.Os and men with the exception of Nos.1 and 2 of Lewis Gun teams, and Signallers, will carry 120 rounds of S.A.A. per man. This ammunition will be drawn from the Quartermaster's Stores tomorrow, 18th instant.
Half the Mobile Reserve of S.A.A., Grenades, and Fireworks will be carried on the busses. The remainder will be carried on the limbers.

3. RETURN. Officers Commanding Companies will render a state to the Orderly Room by 0900 hours daily, showing the expenditure of S.A.A, Grenades etc.

4. EQUIPMENT AND BAGGAGE. The Battalion will move with Equipment and Baggage as laid down in Mobilization Store Table.
Equipment, Clothing and Ordnance Stores, surplus to the above, will be returned to the D.A.D.O.S. Lists in triplicate will be rendered by the Quartermaster by 1000 hours on Thursday, 19th instant.

5. OFFICERS BAGGAGE. Officers valises will not exceed 55 lbs. in weight, and will be carried on the Baggage Wagon. All surplus kit will be removed and securely packed and left with surplus stores.

6. SURPLUS STORES. All Surplus Stores will be stacked at the Quartermaster's Stores tomorrow, 18th inst., ready for conveyance to ENGELSKIRCHEN for storage in the ENGEL FACTORY.
Officer Commanding Details will detail a party for removing this Baggage, and will arrange for a guard to be mounted over them at ENGELSKIRCHEN.
Blankets, which will not be taken forward, will be rolled in bundles of 10 and stacked with the stores. One lorry will report to convey these stores to ENGELSKIRCHEN.
Mess Kits will be limited to one basket per mess.

7. CAMP. The Camp will be left standing, and Officer Commanding Details will detail a guard of 1 N.C.O. and 3 men to look after it. This guard will have 2 days rations and Iron Rations.

8. MEDICAL. "B" Section of 139th Field Ambulance, consisting of 3 Medical Officers and 60 other ranks of R.A.M.C., and 4 Motor Ambulances and Horsed Transport will march with the Main Body of the Brigade Group.
One Motor Ambulance and 4 R.A.M.C. bearers will be attached to the Battalion during the advance and will join the Battalion under arrangements to be made by O.C.Section.
Sick and Casualties will be collected from collecting posts by No.30 M.A.C..

(Sgd) T.P.NEWMAN Captain.
Adjutant 11th Bn "The Queen's" (Royal West Surrey) Regt.

Copies to recipients of Operation Orders.No.6.

SECRET.

COMPOSITION OF BUS COLUMN.

ADVANCED GUARD.

MAIN BODY.

Burgomaster's House,
KNOELSKIRCHEN.

 (8 Busses.   Brigade Headquarters.
 (6 Busses.   One Company 2/4th Bn. Queen's Regt.
 (8 Busses.   "B" Coy. M. Gun Battalion.

Plus 2 Spare Busses.

---

26 Busses.   2/4th Bn. Queen's Regt.
Motor Ambulance. Attd 2/4th Bn. Queen's Regt.
2 Busses.   253rd Field Coy. R.E.
1 Lorry.   "   "   "   "
4 Busses.   T.M.B.

Plus 3 Spare Busses.

---

1 Bus.   Bn. Hdqrs. 11th Bn. Queen's Regt.
7 Busses. Bn. Hdqrs. Coy.   "   "   "
1 Lorry.   With Stores   "   "   "
6 Busses. "A" Coy.   "   "   "
6 Busses. "D" Coy.   "   "   "

Plus 2 Spare Busses.

---

1 Lorry.   Brigade Headquarters.
Motor Ambulance. Attd. 11th Bn. Queen's Regt.

Gap for the 113th Siege Battery R.G.A.

---

1 Bus.   Remainder 122nd F.A. and M.A.

Brigade Supply M.T. Column.

Gap for 187th Brigade R.F.A.

---

6 Busses.   "B" Coy. 11th Bn. Queen's Regt.
       (Escort to R.F.A.)
When relieved by Cavalry will join the column between "A" & "D"
Companies.

Gap for Group 1st Line Transport.
5 Busses.   2 Platoon "C" Coy. 11th Bn. Queen's Regt.
       (Escort to 1st Line Transport).

---

5 Busses.   2 Platoons "C" Coy. 11th Bn. Queen's Regt.
       (REAR GUARD).

T.R.Newman
                Captain.
Adjutant 11th Battalion "The Queen's" (R.W.S) Regt.

S E C R E T.

INSTRUCTIONS TO ACCOMPANY OPERATION ORDER No. 7.
(Dated 17th June 1919).

18th June 1919.

1. Sixteen Magazines per Lewis Gun will be taken on the Busses.

2. Four shovels and 2 picks will be taken by each Company for Sanitary Purposes.

3. Messages will be sent up and down the Column by runners during the halts. The Busses conveying Company Headquarters will be clearly marked.

4. All sentries, guards, also troops employed on Escort Duty will have their magazines charged.

5. All troops will be informed of their position and of the Platoon or Company Alarm Posts.

6. The duties of sentries will be carefully explained to the men, in addition to preventing surprise, they will prevent any civilians entering or leaving a village without an English Pass dated on or after 20th June 1919.

7. Two Verey Pistols, and 12 1" red lights will be issued to each Company, and will be kept by Company Headquarters.

8. All blankets will be rolled in bundles of 10 and securely tied and labelled, and stacked outside the Company Lines facing the road, by 0700 hours tomorrow morning.

9. Officers Commanding "A", "B", "C" and "D" Companies will each detail 5 men to join the Details, to remain behind at ENGELSKIRCHEN. Nominal Rolls of all details being left behind will be forwarded to the Adjutant by 1200 hours tomorrow.

10. The dress for the move will be F.S.M.O.
Steel helmets will be worn, and S.B.Respirators slung.

11. On the busses troops will remove their packs, but will wear the remainder of their equipment.

12. Water Bottles will be filled each morning, and troops will be impressed of the importance of retaining the water as long as possible, owing to the uncertainty of a further supply during the day.

13. Officer Commanding Details will detail a guard of 1 NCO and 3 men to look after the Camp on the Brigade Cricket Ground, ENGELSKIRCHEN on Friday, 20th instant.

(Sgd) T.P. NEWMAN. Captain.
Adjutant 11th Bn "The Queen's" (R.W.S) Regiment.

Copies to all recipients
of Operation Orders

Page 1.

Army Form C. 2118.

WAR DIARY
or
INTELLIGENCE SUMMARY.
(Erase heading not required.)

Ref. Map. Sheet 59 C.W. 1-100,000.

July 1919.

Place	Date	Hour	Summary of Events and Information	Remarks and references to Appendices
EHRESHOVEN	1st		Training and Education during the morning. A & B Coys at Musketry on the range. Afternoon – Recreation.	
	2nd		Do – Do –	
	3rd		A General Holiday was held to celebrate the opening of Peace. Battn Sports were held during the day.	
	4th		A Battn Parade was held at 09.00 hrs in fighting order for Inspection by the Comdg Officer. "B" & "D" Coys commenced firing the General Musketry Course.	
	5th		Training & Education during the morning. C & D Coys at Musketry. Recreation during the afternoon.	
	6th		Divine Service held in the Gardens of the Schloss at 09.15 hrs.	

Page 71

Army Form C. 2118.

WAR DIARY
or
INTELLIGENCE SUMMARY.

(Erase heading not required.) Ref: Area Shut 59 COLN 1-100,000

Place	Date	Hour	Summary of Events and Information	Remarks and references to Appendices
	July 1919			
	7th		The Battalion was inspected by the Divl Comdr. (Ser. S.T.B. Lawford K(CB) at 09.15 hrs. and afterwards at training and musketry.	
	8th		Training and Education in the morning, C. & D Coys at musketry. Afternoon – Recreation.	
	9th		Training, Education, & Bathing in the morning. C & D Coys at musketry. Afternoon – Recreation.	
	10th		Do – Do – Do	
	11th		Training & Education in the morning. C & D Coys completes G.M.C. and Course of A & B Coys commenced firing the Course. Afternoon – Recreation	
	12th		Interior Economy & Inspections in the morning. Canals at Hunerkti Brigade Sports held in afternoon, Balm woo 2nd in Champinship Total 737 rods.	

Page III

Army Form C. 2118.

WAR DIARY
or
INTELLIGENCE SUMMARY.

(Erase heading not required.) Ref. Maps Sheet 59 COLN 1-100,000

JULY 1919.

Place	Date	Hour	Summary of Events and Information	Remarks and references to Appendices
	13th		Divine Service was held in A & B Coys Dining Hut at 09.15hrs	
	14th		Training & Education, and preparing for move to KALK. Cavalry completes musketry course.	
THRESHOVEN	15th		Battalion was relieved by 9th Bn East Surrey Regt and proceeded to THRESHOVEN Station where it entrained at 11.30 hrs, reached KALK and detrained at 14.15 hrs, and occupies billets vacated by 9th East Surrey Regt.	
	16th		The Battalion took over all Guards & Duties in the KALK Area and remainder attends training etc.	
KALK	17th		Training etc carried out during the morning. 21 O.Rs transferred to R.A.M.C. under authority Rhine Army Letter No A/6.3/14/03 of 21.6.19.	

(A9123) Wt W2358/P.60 60,000 12/17 D. D. & L. Sch 52a. Form C2118/15

Page 4.
Army Form C. 2118.

WAR DIARY
or
INTELLIGENCE SUMMARY.

(Erase heading not required.) Ref. Map. Sheet 5G COLN - 1-100,000.

Place	Date	Hour	Summary of Events and Information	Remarks and references to Appendices
	18th		Training & Educational. Carried out during the morning. Recreation in Afternoon.	
	19th		General holiday for celebration of Peace. 28 O.Rs. transferred to Hr. G. Corps under Gine Army Letter N° 613/23 (03) dy- 21.6.19	
	20th		Divine Service was held in the Y.M.C.A. KAISER HOUSE STRASSE at 09.30 hrs	
ITLY	21st		Training & Education relief of Guard. Afternoon Recreation.	
	22nd		Do — Do — Do	
	23rd		Do — Do — Do	

Page 5

Army Form C. 2118.

WAR DIARY
or
INTELLIGENCE SUMMARY

(Erase heading not required.)

Place	Date	Hour	Summary of Events and Information	Remarks and references to Appendices
Ry. Guard. Shed 59. Coln. 1-100,000	July 1919.			
	24th		Training & Education in the morning. Recreation in Afternoon.	
	25th		Do — Do —	
	26th		Training etc. "C" Coy (Capt J.C. Hedley DSO, MC) won the Brigade Coy Competition for efficiency with a total of 211 points.	
	27th		Divine Service was held in Lutheran Church in VICTOR STRASSE KALK at 11.00 hrs.	
	28th		Training & Education. Recreation in Afternoon.	
	29th		Do — Do —	
	30th		Bn relieved of all Guards by 2/4th Bn The Queens Rgt	
	31st		Trained & Educated in the morning.	

for O.C. 11th Bn The Queens Rgt

Army Form C. 2118.

WAR DIARY
or
INTELLIGENCE SUMMARY.
(Erase heading not required.)

Ref. Map - Cologne 1 - 100,000.

August 1919.

Place	Date	Hour	Summary of Events and Information	Remarks and references to Appendices
	1st		Training and Education during the morning. Batho. athletics to "B" "D" Coys & Transport during the afternoon. Kemango at Recreation.	
	2nd		Training from 08.00 to 10.00. Latrine economy from 10.00 to 12.00. Recreation during afternoon.	
	3rd		Divine Service in Protestant Church VICTOR STRASSE, KALK at 11.00 hrs.	
	4th		August Bank Holiday.	
	5th		Training & Education during the morning. Recreation in the afternoon.	
	6th		Battalion parades and proceeds to EXERZIER PLATZ, HOHENBURG and carried out parades for Army Council Reviews. Recreation during the afternoon.	

Army Form C. 2118.

WAR DIARY
or
INTELLIGENCE SUMMARY

(Erase heading not required.)

Instructions regarding War Diaries and Intelligence Summaries are contained in F. S. Regs., Part II. and the Staff Manual respectively. Title pages will be prepared in manuscript.

Map Sheet. Cologne 1-18,000.

August 1919.

Place	Date	Hour	Summary of Events and Information	Remarks and references to Appendices
	7th		The Battalion paraded at 0930 hours and embussed and proceeded to the EXERZIER PLATZ, LONGERICH where a rehearsal for the Army General Review was carried out.	
	8th		Training, Education, & Bathing was carried out by the Battalion.	
	9th		Training & Education Inspector Economy was carried out during the morning. Recreation during the afternoon. Major B.M. Allen M.C. posted to the Battn. as 2nd in Cmd.	
	10th		Divine Service held in BOTOLAND Church VICTOR STR. KALK at 11.00 hrs.	
KALK	11th		Training & Education during the morning, & Recreation during the afternoon.	

WAR DIARY
or
INTELLIGENCE SUMMARY

Army Form C. 2118.

Ref. 4/4/9 Shes - Cologne 1-100,000.

August 1919

Place	Date	Hour	Summary of Events and Information	Remarks and references to Appendices
	12th		The Battalion took part in the General Parade on the EXERZIER PLATZ at 10.15 hrs.	
	13th		Transport Inspection during the morning. Recreation during the afternoon.	
	14th		Do	
	15th		Do	
	16th		Do	— 2 Soldiers leaving	
	17th	11.00 hrs.	Divine Service in Protestant Church VICTOR STRASSE KALK at	
KALK	18th		Battalion paraded at 08.30 hours and proceeded on course to EXERZIER PLATZ, LONGRICH, and took part in the Brigade Route March which was Composed of the VIth Corps.	

Army Form C. 2118.

WAR DIARY
or
INTELLIGENCE SUMMARY.
(Erase heading not required.)

Regt: hrgs - Cologne 1-100.000

August 1919.

Instructions regarding War Diaries and Intelligence Summaries are contained in F. S. Regs., Part II. and the Staff Manual respectively. Title pages will be prepared in manuscript.

Place	Date	Hour	Summary of Events and Information	Remarks and references to Appendices
KÖLN	19th		Training & Education, and hrockety on the Bucks Camp, from 08.00 to 12.00.	
	20th		Training & Education during morning. Recreation during afternoon.	
	21st		Do — Do —	
	22nd		Do — Do —	
	23rd		Do — Do — 1 Sniper Exercise Do —	
	24th		Divine Service in Protestant Church in VICTOR STRASSE KASERNE at 11.00 hrs. Training & Education during the morning. Recreation during the afternoon.	
	25th			

Army Form C. 2118.

WAR DIARY
or
INTELLIGENCE SUMMARY.
(Erase heading not required.)

Ref: Map – Cologne 1:100 000

August 1919.

Place	Date	Hour	Summary of Events and Information	Remarks and references to Appendices
	26th		Training & Education carried out during the morning. Recreation during the afternoon. Adv. Party leaving at Elberhorn.	
	27th		Do	
	28th		Do	
	29th		Battalion took over Kair area Guards from 2/4th Queens.	
	30th		Training & Interior Economy.	
	31st		Church Service in Protestant Church in Victor Strasse at 11.00 hrs	

Montgomerie.
Lieut Colonel
Commanding 11th Bn The Queens Regt

1 Queens

Army Form C. 2118.

WAR DIARY
or
INTELLIGENCE SUMMARY.
(Erase heading not required.)

Ref Map — Cologne 1 : 100000

Month and year: September 1919

Place	Date	Hour	Summary of Events and Information	Remarks and references to Appendices
	1st		Training and Education during morning. "Recreation" in the afternoon. Divisional Sports at POLL.	
	2nd		Training and Education during morning. Afternoon recreation.	
	3rd		do. do.	
POLL	4th		Education for C & B Coys from 0800 to 1200 hrs. A & B Coys and Transport bathed during afternoon.	
POLL	5th		Company Training for C & B Coys at EXERCIER PLATZ during morning.	
	6th		Kit Inspection and Interior Economy (08.00 – 10.30 hrs) and Education (11.00 – 12.00 hrs) for C & B Coys.	

WAR DIARY
or
INTELLIGENCE SUMMARY (Erase heading not required.)

Army Form C. 2118.

Place: Cologne
Ref. map: Cologne 1:100 000
September 1919

Date	Hour	Summary of Events and Information	Remarks and references to Appendices
7th		Divine Service at 11.00 hrs in Protestant Church VICTOR STRASSE.	
8th		Education during the morning for C + D Coys. Company Training for C + D Coys on the EXERCIER PLATZ. This included Outpost Scheme, dispositions for making counter-attacks.	
9th		Morning devoted to Education	
10th		Coy Training on EXERCIER PLATZ in morning	
11th		Education from 08.00 to 12.00 hrs.	
13th		A Battalion Boxing Competition took place during the morning. All men not on duty were present.	

Army Form C. 2118.

WAR DIARY
or
INTELLIGENCE SUMMARY.
(Erase heading not required.)

Place: Map ref. Cologne 1/100,000
Date: September 1919

Place	Date	Hour	Summary of Events and Information	Remarks and references to Appendices
	13th		During the morning a Battalion Bayonet fighting competition was held. The Commanding Officer's Challenge Cup was won by B Coy.	
	14th		The guards found by A & B Coys were relieved during the day by C & D Coys. Divine service was held at 11.00 hrs in the Protestant Church, VICTOR STRASSE.	
ITALK	15th		Company training for A & B Coys on the EXERCIER PLATZ during the morning.	
	16th		London Provisional Horse Show was held today, it being observed as a holiday.	

Army Form C. 2118.

WAR DIARY
or
INTELLIGENCE SUMMARY

(Erase heading not required.)

Place: Cologne
SEPTEMBER 1919
Ref. Map. Cologne 1/100.000

Place	Date	Hour	Summary of Events and Information	Remarks and references to Appendices
	17th		'A' & 'B' Coys carried out field firing. Recreation during afternoon.	
	18th		'A' & 'B' Coys carried out Education during the morning and bathed during the afternoon.	
	19th		Field training carried out by 'A' & 'B' Coys during the morning. Recreation during the afternoon.	
	20th		Interior Economy & Education during the morning. Recreation during the afternoon.	
	21st		'A' & 'B' Coys relieved the Guard furnished by 'C' & 'D' Coys. Church Service was held at 11.00 hr. for the remanded in the Protestant Church in VICTOR STRASSE.	

27417

WAR DIARY
or
INTELLIGENCE SUMMARY

Army Form C. 2118.

(Erase heading not required.) Reg Head - Cologne 1-100,000

September 1919

Place	Date	Hour	Summary of Events and Information	Remarks and references to Appendices
	22nd		C. & D. Coys carried out Field Training on EXERZIER PLATZ, HOHENBURG during the morning. Recreation during the afternoon.	
	23rd		C. & D. Coys carried out Education, and recreation in the afternoon.	
	24th		C. & D. Coys carried out Field Training. D. Coy carried out an Outpost Scheme. Recreation during the afternoon.	
	25th		Education carried out during the morning. Recreation during the afternoon.	
	26th		Field Training (Scheme) carried out by C. & D. Coys. Baths during the afternoon.	

Army Form C. 2118.

WAR DIARY
or
INTELLIGENCE SUMMARY

(Erase heading not required.)

Place: Ref. Map. Cologne 1-100,000

Date: September 1919

Place	Date	Hour	Summary of Events and Information	Remarks and references to Appendices
	27th		C. & D. Coys carried out Interior Economy during the morning. Recreation during the afternoon.	
	28th		Divine Service in Protestant Church, VICTOR STR. at 11.00 hours.	
	29th		'C' & D' Coys fatties and all clothing & belts inspected.	
	30th		C. & D. relieves A & B Coys of all Guards.	

J.P. Newman Lt/Major
Comdg 11th Bn "The Queens" R.

www.ingramcontent.com/pod-product-compliance
Lightning Source LLC
Chambersburg PA
CBHW080855230426
43662CB00013B/2112